So... When Do I See the Doctor?

A Rx for Treating Chronic Marginalization
While Preserving Yourself Through It All

Kimberly Gilbert, MD

as told to Chrishaunda Lee Perez

DH Book Consulting & Publishing
McDonough, Georgia

Published by DH Book Consulting & Publishing
100 Postmaster Drive #3235
McDonough, GA 30253
www.dhbooksandpublishing.com

Cover Design by Shan Mark
Editing by Nicole Allen
Photography by Drexina Nelson Photography

Printed in the United States of America

First Printing: 2020

ISBN: 978-1-7334436-6-1

For my beautiful girls, who inspire me every day to be and give my best —
Never lose your curiosity, creativity, and enthusiasm.
Keep asking "Why?" and never take, "Because, that's how it is." for the answer.
God could not have given me a greater gift than the opportunity to be your mother.
I pray He protects and guides you throughout your amazing lives.
No matter where your journeys take you,
you will always have a home in my heart.
There is no mistake, no disagreement, no decision that will ever change that.
And when I am gone, I hope you understand that while I was on this earth,
I ran my leg of the race the best I could before handing the baton over to you.
Stay smart, stay strong, stay YOU.

Foreword

It has been my absolute pleasure and delight to read through this memoir. To say that Dr. Gilbert's experiences and writing incited so many emotions for me is an understatement. Aside from the fact that I got to learn that we have so much more in common than originally known, I can relate wholeheartedly to her experience. In her depictions, she accomplished the difficult task of conveying her experience so very vividly. One can be from a very different way of life, experience, or perspective, and if they are truly willing to understand, they will. While reading, I cried, laughed, got angry and even stopped for moments of reflection as some of the parts took me back to my personal trauma of dealing with racists, condescending, under-mining individuals that I've had to deal with on my journey. Unfortunately, her experience — our shared experience — is shared by so many more, especially those sisters who chose a path similar to ours and are black women physicians.

Our plight has not been easy, but by writing this book, she has used her journey as a tool to reach back and give; especially for our younger sisters coming up behind us. The impact of this project will be so profound! To say I'm proud of her is an under-statement. Her courage is impeccable, and I'm honored to call her friend.

As you go on the journey in this book, you'll find that it is brilliantly written; personal, but yet very relatable. This book helps to bring a sense of clarity to those who have endured similar experiences, and serves as a professional blueprint for those who, unfortunately, will.

— Dr. Sarepta Isaac

Contents

Introduction

You are not good enough.

What you think or feel doesn't matter because you don't matter.

Why? Simply because you are you…

Feeling the traumatic blow of being disempowered, excluded, marginalized, devalued, or outright ignored, is something no one ever wants to experience. But more often than not, so many people will go through a period of being able to check one of these boxes of unfair treatment.

Are you an athlete whose intellect is often downplayed? An attractive woman who often gets mistaken for a lower level employee and not the boss? LGBTQ (lesbian, gay, bisexual, transgender and queer)? A person of color? If so, there is no question whether at some point in your life you will feel the effects of not being valued.

I happen to check two boxes of our world's most marginalized and commonly treated unfairly; Black and Female. Despite this fact though, by the truest characteristics which historically and currently define us — our strength and courage — we Black women do not succumb to any level of adversity. Moreover, there are those of us comprising this group who, time after time, have risen to levels of professional and social excellence by also conquering other marginalized aspects of humanity like being poor and undereducated. Black women, throughout our world's history in various roles — regardless of where we come from — have showcased that we are indeed capable.

There are immeasurable numbers of Black women leaders and innovators who prove what I am telling you. You might know this, too. It is unfortunate though, that many of us will graduate at or near the top of our class, aspire and succeed in careers that yield financial stability or great wealth, and still be treated in a manner beneath all of our achievements. Everyone, regardless of what we look like, what we do for a living, or how much money we make should be treated with respect.

We are good enough, and we do matter.

The world often shows more appreciation for those we see on television or in the movies. As many wise people have said, "The most important person is the one you need right now." This could be your physician, your accountant, your babysitter, or the janitor in your apartment building. Each person has value. Each person deserves respect, and no one should be misprized. Yet, at alarming rates, no matter what career or work title we hold, Black women are disrespected and undervalued. It could be due to another person choosing to project their insecurities onto us — either because we have risen to a level of success they hoped to have achieved, or resentment because someone has to view us as a peer or colleague and not someone subordinate to them. I do know that it has nothing to do with the quality of our work. For medical professionals like me, our bedside manner and level of expertise can be exemplary. But regardless of the industry, the marginalization Black women experience often has everything to do with characteristics that are purely external and nothing to do with who we are as people or the quality of the services we provide.

So... When Do I See the Doctor?

I am a physician, and I specialize in Physical Medicine and Rehabilitation. My formal title is Physiatrist. Like all medical doctors, my job entails interacting with and serving people of many races and cultures. I spend long hours caring for those young, old, and in between. I aspired to be a part of the healthcare industry because a core tenant in the medical world is helping others, which was instilled in me early in my childhood. I also grew up loving science, and so manifesting these influences into the study of medicine was quite natural for me. I worked hard from earning my place in medical school to attaining the leadership positions I hold for the work I do today.

With the diverse patient ethnicities and nationalities that I serve, being a Black doctor who is also a woman makes for an interesting combination. I am fortunate to know many other healthcare professionals who are also Black, and so my village feels like there are many of us around even if we do not work in the same buildings. In reality, Black physicians make up a very small percentage of the total number of physicians in the United States (and throughout the world), and approximately 2% of current physicians in the United States are Black females.[1]

These solemn statistics are one of the many reasons I am often misperceived or mislabeled as being a nurse, nurse's aide, or anything other than a physician — regardless of what my name tag says.

This leads me to addressing stereotyping. If you are typecast in any form, it might be challenging for others to see you in a different light, for societal norms train the mentalities of people. And unless those people are open to exercising free-thinking, you might fall victim to their controlled way of seeing the world. Black people in general, suffer from being on the unfair end of negative stereotypes about us by society almost every day of our lives. In addition to earning the credentials to serve in a certain profession, many of us must still prove to others we deserve the positions we have earned. Because of this "societal-trained" mentality, it is sometimes difficult to believe that the Black man or woman you are engaging with at a corporation is in charge of it all. Furthermore, it might be confusing to grasp that between the two women assigned to lead a class, the one not of color is the teacher assistant.

Then, there are the gray areas. In my line of work, being a woman of color does not have to be such a damning thing — if you are the "right" sort of color. If I were Asian or Middle Eastern, perhaps a patient or fellow medical professional not familiar with me would give me the benefit of the doubt and assume that I am the physician and not say things to me like they will hold their questions for "the doctor" after I (the presumed medical assistant, nurse, or nurse's aide) had finished my encounter. But I am Black, and so there is less chance I will receive that kind of grace. I cannot fully express how many times a patient will half-listen to me — not believing the buck stops with me— only to have to ask the same questions twice when they learn that I, Dr. Kimberly Gilbert, am the physician, and not the nurse. In years past, I became clever and would have my medical assistant write all of the important points as I spoke, so when a patient felt at a loss because they had not paid attention to my recommendations, they were sent home with the written key points. This way, the patient could still be well informed and, at the same time, not feel embarrassed. I will be "over the moon" when we see the day people believe what they read on the name tag.

In the following pages, you will learn about my life; from its modest beginning through failures and successes. I have been through enough of a life's journey thus far not to feel too shy to share; all my experiences bring me nothing but pride and joy. Why would you care to read about all of this? Because I know I am not alone in my feelings of reaching the limit for tolerating being marginalized. You do not have to look like me or be in my line of work to have these feelings about a career in which you have worked hard to succeed, only to be belittled. You can check almost any box of "other," and you will find yourself with a similar, if not heightened, level of frustration. This book is not about being discouraged or lending all of one's energy to frustration. It is about celebrating a journey of triumph despite being overlooked, bringing awareness to a chronic inequity in which our culture could use a swift and potent antidote of healing, and an overall realization about how to appreciate the value of every human being who is contributing to our world.

I hope my story inspires you to share it with others and have serious conversations about it with your family and friends, neighbors, colleagues and co-workers, or anyone you feel could benefit from awareness. If you can relate to my story, I hope it gives you the courage to bring this awareness to your supervisors and co-workers, for they are not always cognizant of the challenges we face in a work environment. Enlightening them about what you might be going through can help move those who support you to action. I believe that no closed mouth gets fed, and no true healing can happen without getting to the deepest layer of the scar. However difficult it may be, this is the only way to catalyze real change.

PART ONE

— *THE ROOTS* —

1

My Village

"A tree's beauty lies in its branches, but its strength lies in its roots."
- Matshona Dhliwayo

My parents never told me what I should or should not become in life. Their parenting priority was to groom me to be successful in whatever life I chose to live. I consider them the greatest human beings who walked the earth because of it. They gave me the freedom of choice while still being the most impactful guides in my life. Intelligence and academic excellence were emphasized for my older sister and me (today, my big sister, Ericka, serves as an attorney). For my parents, being "intelligent" did not mean we only made good grades; it meant understanding how to use the knowledge we gained to help us make the most informed decisions while also planting an eagerness for lifelong learning.

My parents instilled many ideals and values throughout my childhood, key among them being the abilities to prioritize responsibilities and not procrastinate. "Get the work done now so you can have fun later." are sentiments I heard from each of them at various times growing up. My father was a coach and my mother taught high school Biology and Chemistry. My parents were full of wisdom — knowing what to do and when to do it. I watched them juggle seasonal sports games, summer practices, and off-season training while also grading quizzes and tests, and creating detailed lesson plans every week throughout the school year. This, all while keeping two curious daughters in check. And it did not end there. The Gilbert household, with our garden, the horses and almost every other farm animal you could imagine, was always filled with things to do and a certain time it had to be done.

Ericka and I were taught that life should involve productive and purposeful things to do. On school days, after practice we would go home and complete our homework. But after that, there were tasks to complete that did not result in a "grade" from a teacher, but more "approval" from mom or dad. Sundays were dedicated to church in the morning and watching football, or watching and playing basketball, in the afternoon. Our parents were a great team. They wisely decided between each other, when advising or correcting us, who would be best in the moment to make the final "head coach" decision.

Daddy was the tough, dedicated, and passionate football and basketball coach who helped many boys and girls at his school and in the surrounding area. Some would say he played surrogate father to many of those who often came from single-mother homes. My dad understood his important role in the lives of the kids he mentored. It is true that some of them would have had little, if any other positive Black male influence at arm's length if it were not for my dad choosing to be there. Not only did he coach these kids, but he also gave them things to do to keep them out of trouble. Many times, he even took them for a hot meal after practice.

In his near fifty-year career as a coach, I witnessed many of these interactions as he showed great care for so many young people. Sometimes we would be in the basketball gym, and other times in our yard or driveway. My mom would look out at us from the kitchen window while cooking and never complain. She understood. There was no specific rhyme or reason for doing all of this, except that my dad believed in those he helped. His belief meant that his support for them could not be contained to the school grounds. He would also allow a student's younger sibling to tag along if it meant the student could not participate in an activity without them, or if it would potentially keep the younger sibling out of trouble. My dad wished for no one to be left behind, and this care was not for the purpose of him simply trying to fill a role. The students, who ranged from elementary to high school knew it, too. They valued the sincerity and dedication my dad showed them every day. When he passed on, my dad's ceremony was jam-packed with family, friends, colleagues, and an astound-ing number of the former students he mentored — proving how much he meant to so many kids.

Dad had served for such a long time at his school and at the neighborhood recreation center, that many of his later stu-dents were the children of students he had coached earlier in his career. In the boys, I believe Dad saw himself in certain ways. And in the girls, I believe he considered them to be extensions of Ericka and me who were also deserving of as much support as he could provide. Dad's intervention was meant to help guide a positive future for them. Under his lead, many more than my sister and I grew up and did well in life.

Ericka and I were little girls when we began witnessing and experiencing all of this, and Dad pulled no punches with us, raising Ericka and me with the same level of grit-inspiring lessons. We might have worn ponytails with bows, but we learned to fall and get back up on our own. From Dad, we learned how to self-soothe, and we got our hands dirty. A lot. A familiar quote of my dad's while growing up was, "Imma let you bump your head so next time you know to duck."

Dad drove a pickup truck that he let Ericka and me help him paint a copper-brown color. He loved it. I will never forget how pleased he was with the outcome. It was in the back of that truck that I spent many moments daydreaming about life and all it could hold for me in my young mind. At one point, my dad also coached us in sports, and through it we developed a great deal of resilience. There were times in junior high school when I felt I did not perform the best I could have, and with my personality, it was hard for me to let the "supposed failure" go. Dad would know how to respond, offering me an opportunity to get right what I thought was wrong until I received closure. Sometimes I needed to shoot baskets until I thought my shot was stronger. Sometimes I needed a pep talk. After a home game was over and everyone else was gone, he would turn the lights in the gym back on and let me work on anything I felt I did wrong earlier in the game. As opposed to letting things get the best of me, I learned how to channel my energy in the direction that would make me better. It was my dad who encouraged me to dream big but to be sure to "do the work" to get there.

But Dad was not all rough and tumble. I watched how, like with us, he would care for a baby animal being born. He would give them treatments such as antimicrobial baths in huge tubs and create formulas to supplement the milk some of the mothers could not produce, doing his best to focus on any detail in the earliest part of their lives. He believed that it was at those vital moments of life when any living thing could be either broken down or fortified at the root, depending on what care was given. It was important for my dad to help any living thing or person get on a solid track at the earliest stage he could for them. Like trees, fortified rooting within people and animals helps them grow strong, while frail roots result in them becoming feeble and uncertain. On my daddy's watch, his girls had strong roots, his plants and animals had strong roots, and he hoped to have intervened at the right time for the boys and girls who he mentored so they could have strong roots as well.

At home, Dad could be heard waking up Ericka and me each morning with one of his favorite songs, "Mornin', Mr. Radio," by Al Jarreau. He sang that song so often I can hear his melody in my ears now...Dad would perform that tune down the hall leading to our bedrooms to greet us with a smile. We knew it was time to get up, brush our teeth, get dressed, eat breakfast, and get to the business of the day.

Dad took us everywhere with him. Some of our girl-friends remained indoors to keep scrapes off their legs, but Dad did not raise us to be "inside children." He taught me how to run his tilling machine when I could barely see over it. Standing in front of him with my feet on top of his, both of us holding onto the handles, he would let me run it up and down the field. Steering was first, and then as I got taller, he taught me to operate the whole thing. And of the many fruit trees and bushes we had around — apple, fig, blackberry, strawberry, and plum — we were taught how to properly nurture and harvest them so we could later help Mom make jam from scratch. Dad even instructed me on how to keep the wild animals and pesky bugs from infiltrating our crops. Even after tackling homework and other after-school activities, completing daily yardwork, gardening, and household chores along with weekly piano lessons, my dad would still ask us, "Now, who wants to help me build something?" to which we would immediately shout, "ME!"

When on our own, Ericka and I hung out a lot with some of the students he mentored, and they often gave us "big kid" wisdom to avoid mistakes they had made. Spending time with the older guys and girls felt like the most comfortable thing. Yes, we still played with dolls, but we gravitated to the empowered ones like Wonder Woman and She Ra, Princess of Power. No surprise there.

I think my dad wanted us to be exposed to as much as he could show us because he knew that one day he would not be there, and at least we could get a lot of practice and experience under his watchful eye. His faithful pickup truck we helped paint and, I affectionately called "Buddy" (because of how much time I rode in him), held at times a squad of boys and girls in the back, including Ericka and me. Daddy did not have us sit in front with him away from the boys. He wanted us to spend time around them early so we could get familiar with them and understand them. He encouraged them to understand girls as well; another reason why he mentored boys and girls alike. I thank my dad for having us in a safe environment to engage with the opposite sex so young. The boys looked up to our dad (as well as had a healthy fear of him) so they treated us like little sisters.

I attribute the strong friendships I now have with men that have nothing to do with us being involved in a romantic relationship, to the influence of my dad. He showed us how to connect while keeping our priorities straight. He always felt that it was extremely important to be respected by boys and men, and I believe I have always felt that way because of how my dad emphasized us being around them. Even with the solid relationship I have with my husband, I owe much of my contribution to that relationship to my dad, who showed my sister and me by example what a dedicated and loving father and husband looks like.

My dad's rearing also prepared me for life in medicine, which is dominated by men. My lack of intimidation by men throughout medical school, residency and beyond — even when I was the only female in the room — might have inspired a few resentful male colleagues. Nevertheless, in the end, they had no choice but to respect me because I was not intimidated, and I had my act together.

Walking across the stage to receive my degree from medical school, I did two things: first, I peered into the audience and locked eyes with my mother and sister; then I averted my eyes upward to salute my dad who was not alive to watch me graduate. Still, I felt his spirit immensely. Dad knew he would not be here forever, but he made sure he set me up perfectly for my life after he was gone.

Looking back, I realize that my parents' roles were not "gender-based," especially for that time. While my dad taught us sports and other outdoor activities, one of those outdoor activities was gardening. Dad was the tough guy who also serenaded his daughters to wake us up each morning, and regardless of how strong a demeanor he portrayed as one of the male pillars in our community, he often showed a soft side. Mom, who might have been assumed to be the softy simply because she was a woman, like Dad, took on a multi-layered role with us as well. Dad's lessons were tender but tough. Mom's lessons were tough but tender.

You may wonder if there was time left for our mother to contribute a solid and consistent handle on us, as it could seem that most of our time was spent with Dad. Where Dad dominated in real-life teachings outdoors and socially, Mom was our academic and "Indoor General".

Like Dad, Mom was very intelligent. She taught science to high schoolers and was my first real example that a woman could pursue a career in science and still have a family. I do not know how I could have been blessed with a better scenario. Mom was stern and direct because she had to be. Like my experiences in a world overwhelmed with male practitioners, I can imagine how often my mother was told she should pursue teaching something more "female" such as home economics, rather than chemistry and biology. Mom was a rare bird for the time because she was a Black woman who taught science, and in two concentrations of it.

With words, my dad instilled into me why I should not be intimidated by men, but my mom showed me how not to be intimidated by being herself. Her toughness was exemplified by how on-point she always was. And because she was a woman of science, her passion was, in most points, backed by proven facts. I can imagine how aware my mother had to be about her smiles, sense of humor, and vulnerable moments in the workplace, lest someone could take her kindness, or softness, as a weakness. My mother was a fair and balanced woman who accomplished a difficult achievement during that time in our country. She hit a ceiling because in my profession today, I know that my mother had the intellect to become one of our nation's great scientists. In many ways, I feel that my career as a physician is in salute to her as I picked up where she left off.

Mom pushed Ericka and me just so we would follow her example. While she never told us what we should become, she urged and commanded us to read and acquire knowledge. I spent my summers outside with Dad doing some of everything with my hands, but I also read a library's worth of books. Mom had me reading everything from the classics to sciences. As a child, after our elementary school let out for the day, the bus would drop us off at the high school where she taught. While we waited for the high school day to end, Mom would let Ericka and me do age-appropriate experiments in her laboratory, as long as we did not blow up anything. My mom opened my mind to the wonders of science and how much the field can help people and the world in general. I was always fascinated with all the things she taught me in her classroom. And ohhh the day she brought the game "Operation" into our home! I was maybe seven years old. I was so wowed by how one tiny wrong move could affect a "surgery." I realized then how precise science and medicine had to be. I worked hard to insert or remove an organ into or out of the plastic man's body during my "life-saving procedures" without the game buzzer going, "Bzzzz!"

While running errands with Mom, Ericka and I often asked for a toy in the store. My mom's rule was, "Yes" to buying us a toy, but that "toy" had to be a book. This is one way she inspired us to read so much. We treated books with the enthusiasm of toys; over the years we acquired and read scores of them.

Mom showed us real-world experiences at home by giving us chores to do. I was "the vacuumer," and Ericka "ruled the dishes". Mom also taught us how to cook and pay close attention to what and how we were cooking so we didn't burn anything and ensured that the meal tasted "TA-DAA!" Through food, we learned the art of doing something right the first time, so you don't have to do it over. "Don't be indolent or negligent," Mom would remind us. Science also required this level of focus and attention. With Dad, if we missed a shot or did not correctly execute a play during basketball practice, we would have to run "suicides" until we got it right. We had to go up and down the court multiple times until he told us to stop. With Mom, the same repetitive approach applied with the skills she taught us. In quick fashion, Ericka and I evolved into fast learners.

Mom was also our disciplinarian; she was the easier choice between the two. It would have been hard for Dad to transition from serenading us to spanking us. Even when Mom felt the need to — which many times required us picking our own "Mom-approved" belt from the closet or switch from a tree — she would (try to) soften the blow with these words, "You will understand when you get older." Today I am older and yes, I understand, and I am grateful to her. I am not certain about being thankful for the spankings, but for the reason behind them. Her discipline helped shape the woman I am today.

Despite her toughness, Mom had her soft side as well. Her tenderness was exhibited through the great deal of patience she had while allowing us to be hands-on, "under her" in the kitchen and in other areas. Oftentimes she could have rushed food preparation and cooking because she was tired after a long day at work. However, Mom wanted us to be involved, to understand how to prepare meals, and to understand the proper steps it took to do things right the first time.

So... When Do I See the Doctor?

When Dad took us fishing at the lake on the weekends, there was always a clear distinction between the large fish he caught, and the microscopic ones reeled in by Ericka and me. Once home, Dad would unveil all the fish to be filleted, and Mom would carry on as if our popcorn fish were the heartiest fish she'd ever seen! We would sit around the table after Mom cooked them all, and she would go on and on about how proud she was of our little bite-sized fish. Tender.

Throughout my life, my mother served as a beacon of courage and no-nonsense for me. We butted heads a lot in my teenage years. Regardless of how much we had our differences, I could not get through my day without hearing her voice at least one time. Even after I left home for college, I called every evening in order to hear her ask me how I was doing, if I needed anything, or what I ate that day to give her peace of mind that I was okay. My mother was a constant for me. She was front row and center with my sister for my graduation from medical school, though my dad had recently passed away. Yet, by the time I had completed my medical residency, I had neither of my parents waiting in the wings. Ericka, and my future husband, John, held it down for them both.

While in residency in Atlanta, my mother's health had deteriorated at a rapid pace, and due to my grueling schedule at Emory, I was unable to visit her as often as Ericka could with her more flexible schedule. During my time in residency, while my mom grew weaker, somehow, I became stronger. I feel like she, at that time, was sending me everything she had spiritually so I could finish strong. I, for sure, picked up where Mom left off in a committed way.

Another incredible quality about my mom that I follow in her footsteps with my own daughters, was her inclination to expose us to added "She-Roes". She showed my sister and me, in many ways, how to be a complete woman. In addition to Mom, we also had Aunt Tru, Aunt Fritz, Aunt Louise, Grandma Howard, and Mrs. Hadnot, who made the most memorable impressions on me.

Truvesta Johnson, or "Aunt Tru," was my mom's Ace and "sister." They were best friends, and their closeness made it almost impossible for others to discern that they were not related. Aunt Tru also had a daughter, Shae, and both Mom and Aunt Tru treated all of us as though we belonged to them both. To this day, I can call on my Aunt Tru for anything. Aunt Tru was a teacher like Mom, and she also had a no-nonsense attitude when it came to education. She was also a "lady's lady." She instilled in me a wealth of knowledge about keeping a household and many old-school traditions. Aunt Tru was so "traditional lady-like" for that time, always so elegant in a beautiful skirt or dress, often one she had made herself. I was thirty years old the first time I witnessed her wear a pair of pants. Yes, she loved clothes and could make almost anything. Aunt Tru made all my prom and pageant dresses, and she even taught me as a child how to sew dresses for my dolls. A complete package like my mom, Aunt Tru could dress, was smart, and could cook too! The only rivals to my mom's dishes were a few dishes that I must admit Aunt Tru "put her foot in it" more and reigned supreme: hot water cornbread, tea cakes, and German chocolate cake. I'd bet on these in Vegas.

So... When Do I See the Doctor?

Aunt Tru's mother, Grandma Howard, was my grandmother-in-residence. She was head of the Usher Board and meant a lot to our family. My dad's parents had passed away, and my mom's parents lived in Mississippi, so we only saw them once or twice a year. We spent time with Grandma Howard several times a week because she babysat us many days until we entered kindergarten. How to describe Grandma Howard? The best way I can paint a fair picture of Grandma Howard is through moments with her, like sitting with her eating mouth-watering collard greens and hot water cornbread at the table, a game show on the TV in the background, and her gazing at me with a proud look for no reason. Then, there were those times when I felt bad about something, she sat me on her lap, wrapped her arms around me, and rocked. In that moment, any of my little childhood problems would disappear. Grandma Howard was like a soft place to land whenever I needed her.

I had no idea, or even knew that I needed to know, what it took to become an entrepreneur. My mom's friend, Mrs. Hadnot, however, showed me what it meant for a Black woman to be in charge of her own business destiny. I run my businesses with as much focus, skill, and strategy as I watched her run hers. Mrs. Hadnot was a hairstylist who had a salon in her front yard. She shampooed and styled hair for many people around our community; us included. I learned the art of folding my ears down so they would not get burned during Mrs. Hadnot's weekly "press-and-curl" with the hot comb. She was always in control and showed herself to be a trailblazer. She knew how to manage clientele, and everyone felt well attended to. She was not a physician, but she had an impeccable "bedside manner". With her, I also got a head start on the importance of managing the health and look of my hair.

My style influence did not end with my mom, Aunt Tru and Mrs. Hadnot. My favorite aunt on my dad's side, Aunt Fritz, was everything! She was also one of the women who emphasized the importance of being well-groomed. She was charming, smart, stylish, athletic, and took great care of herself. She dazzled when she entered a room, owning her flair, as she was the embodiment of fierce. Aunt Fritz was my personal Diana Ross, and I adored her. She was busy but never hesitated to make time for Ericka and me when we visited her and our other family members who lived in Ohio. As a child, I would melt in her arms the moment we embraced. I could sit for hours listening to her talk. She was known for speaking the truth and had no time for those who did not. Aunt Fritz doted on us without abandon, and I welcomed every bit of it.

Somehow my mother had the vision to bring all these other vital and necessary energies to our lives, from the very beginning, through such a powerful village of women. These were women, who embraced us as their own, and those like Aunt Tru, who are still alive today to watch over us. Beyond the blessing of Aunt Tru always being so "true," she evokes the spirit of my mother when I need it the most.

Last, but not least, my mom's baby sister, Louise, represented a constant "sweetness" for me. What she taught me began when I was her little "Mush Mouse," yet, Aunt Louise's influence was most felt with one single act of love when I grew to be an adult.

Being younger than my mom, I remember Aunt Louise being responsible but fun. Seeing her each time we traveled to

Mississippi to visit our grandparents was always a treat. As a child, I remember my mom had to stand in the gap for Aunt Louise. Once an adult, I understood better this beauty of a big sister stepping in for her little sister. I too have been on the receiving end of this sort of blessing because Ericka has been there for me on many occasions. Years later, when my mother became ill, it was Aunt Louise who stood in the gap the most for my mother, her big sister, and moved my mother in with her while I was still in residency and Ericka was fulfilling her duties in her early years serving as an attorney. Aunt Louise was my mother's caregiver until my mom was called Home. I am forever indebted to her and how easily she responded to the call, with the mindset of, "My big sister was there for me, and I will be there for her." My lessons learned as a child from Aunt Louise were to be kind, honest, and firm in your beliefs. As an adult, those lessons grew to add, "Always be there for those you love."

I witnessed these and many other valuable traits, such as grace and humility, in all those women I have mentioned. As a practicing physician, I realize how essential these traits are to being an effective leader. I learned that listening is more powerful than talking and that showing is often more effective than telling. These women also taught me on so many levels what it means to have the blessing of sisterhood. Each of the "She-Roes" from my childhood represents a different character pillar for me, and I am grateful to them for being such solid and integrity-driven human beings.

I believe both my mother and father are resting in peace knowing that with their guidance, along with the wisdom to surround me with a trusted committee of family and friends, my roots were indeed fortified and capable of withstanding any storms to come.

2

You are Not Smart Enough to be a Doctor

My inquisitive and eager maturing lion-cub, but not-yet valiant lioness ears, shifted to readjust after those cruel words bulleted inside of them as if they were shot through the barrel of a hunter's gun. I imagine today, his beady eyes peering through the gun's peep hole. I was so caught off guard that the armor my parents and surrounding village had been solidifying over the years did not capture the spoken malice in its shield and deflect it. Those callous words, grouped together to produce such a heartless statement, forged a nest inside of me that would take up residence, haunting me for a long time: YOU ARE NOT SMART ENOUGH TO BE A DOCTOR.

My junior year chemistry class had just given our visiting speaker, also a previous graduate of my high school, an animated round of applause. I could not take my eyes off him, reminding myself that Keith Amos was indeed real. My high school chemistry class, White and Black students alike, were in awe of him. He was an impressive young Black man who had risen from our city in Louisiana to attend Harvard Medical School. His presentation was inspiring and so "on the ground relatable" that he made us feel like we could be right where he was if we worked hard, earned the right grades, and kept our eyes on the prize. I knew I had worked hard at doing those things. Since my amazement at what I first understood about medicine through the game of "Operation," the thought of being an actual physician grew more from an idea to a belief in myself that I held securely to my chest. My mother introduced me to the world of science when I was young, and later learning about an extension of it — Medicine — blew my mind. I was not quite sure what kind of physician I wanted to become, for there was a time I wanted to be a Veterinarian because of my endearing love for animals, but that interest later waned. Still, I held "Dr. Gilbert" as a title in my head and heart. Keith Amos made me realize how true that title could and would be.

Keith explained his own life goals, sharing his highs and lows with us teen hopefuls with a smile. Just as fluid as he shook our hands after he concluded, I waltzed myself up to my Chemistry teacher, Mr. George, like I was already wearing my personalized lab coat and affirmed my dream to him. Never having told a soul about my deepest career passion, I proclaimed, "Wow! That was amazing! He is amazing! Someday, I am going to be a doctor." I was almost shocked at myself. In this class, I was not a bench warmer, but I also did not play a starter role. I was reserved and spoke only if I had something to say. No doubt today, I truly did. I stood back, allowing for my teacher to take in my declaration, certain that he would agree with me because, after all, I was raised by a high school chemistry teacher and so the subject had become part of my DNA. I was a strong student. Instead, he smirked. "You? You are not smart enough to be a doctor!"

With that, I was dismissed, not from class, but from my teacher's realm of attention. He did not hold a gaze upon me because I suppose he did not think much of me in the first place. As soon as he gave me his cutting opinion, he was already on to the next student, smiling at whatever they had chosen to share with him.

Walking away, I felt stunned. In all my years, I had never received this level of abasement. I was a multi-sport athlete and was not immune to critique or even losing a game. I had learned how to move past and grow from missing a shot that could have won a game. My parents had taught and encouraged me early in life how to gain closure from a supposed "failure." My grades were not perfect, but I was averaging a 3.5 grade point average (GPA). With my athletic skills and educational strengths, I was known throughout the school and community as being a well-rounded scholar. How could this teacher say such a thing to me? Had he not heard about me over the years? Did I need to show him my full transcript to date to ensure him I was smart enough? That I also had the perseverance to succeed in medical school, just like the future "Doctor" Keith Amos? I did not know Keith well enough to tell him all these things about myself so he could approach Mr. George on my behalf and prove to him that I, too, could be a doctor someday.

Later, I was informed that Mr. George told other students they would make great doctors. Students with a higher grade than me in the class, as well as those with lower grades.

Throughout the day, I replayed in my head why he would say such a thing to me. In an effort to get the critical monkey off my back, I began to question his intent because, where I grew up, all the elders, especially those who looked like me, made it their business to only encourage and support a child's dream. Not squash it.

If it was not me who had the issue, maybe it was him.

At that time, I thought, "What kind of bad day was he

having?"

"What was it about me that threatened him?"

"Why did he feel the need to be so judgmental about the dream of a teenage girl who otherwise only showed promise?"

"What insecurities did he have to impose this feeling of not being enough on me?"

My sixteen-year-old mind's critique of him did not last and quickly reverted to me.

"What did I have to do to be smart enough in his eyes to be a doctor?"

Over the years, this question often kicked me in my gut until I earned my medical degree and finished residency. My completion was a triumph! However, I still question the kind of person who imposes this type of anxiety on a young mind that can oftentimes derail the successful course they were on. Acquiring the ability to excel in the face of trauma is not an ideal way to go, but it is the only choice for many of us. On the other hand, I also feel that succeeding while having your hand held can often make you ill-prepared for inevitable challenges you will have to face alone. Adults, especially parents, should help guide and nurture a child's dream then allow them to go at it with their own tenacity. Teachers, people who take an unofficial oath in their career to be lifters of children's spirits, are out of line when they renege on this promise. A great coach or teacher is supposed to help each young person build their own road map or own game plan that leads toward success. I know what this dynamic looks like because I watched my parents do this with their own students and athletes throughout their careers. I watched my dad take "not star" athletes who wanted to shine in their own ways and create unique game plans that would help them reach their personal goals. I heard the stories from many of my mom's students who might not have excelled academically, about how she went the extra mile to help them become the best student they could be. In my chemistry class, I was not the top student in the class, but I was a solid student. My grades were fine, not exceptional, about a B average. When I expressed my aspirations to Mr. George, his response should have echoed a commitment to help me follow in the footsteps of Keith Amos.

When I was "dismissed" by my teacher, I went cold in his class. For the occasional times I raised my hand in his class to speak up, I turned numb and became muted. Mr. George did not protest. I was no longer serious about the class and did only what was required to pass. Since he thought so little of me anyway, I figured, why bother trying? In hindsight, I realize so many kids are, without mercy, berated, put down, or even ignored by teachers and other adults. As a result, many of these kids give up, fulfilling the prophecy of the mal-intentioned comments and behavior of those whose role should be to keep them going. I was fortunate the rest of my grades were always strong so this flub in Mr. George's class was not going to hurt me. Because it was chemistry, I felt it necessary to share with my mom the unfavorable grade I knew to anticipate, lest she believe like the cobbler's children who have no shoes, I had become the science teacher's scientifically inept daughter.

When I divulged to my mother my impending grade in chemistry, she did not give me grief about it. I trivialized it to me not being able to "get" a certain part of the course concepts in the time allotted at school, but promised that I would study hard over the summer and be sure to catch up the next year. As usual, she trusted my word. I did not share with my mom — the high-standard high school chemistry and biology teacher — the reason why I had fallen behind and become so withdrawn in class was because my high school chemistry teacher, a Black man, who by description could have been an uncle-figure and one of my key male village members, was instead a pessimist, a dream-killer, and a hater. Had my mother known this, Lord knows what she would have done, but I had a strong clue. She would "give him his issue."

T oday, wearing my personalized lab coat emblazoned with "Dr. Kimberly Gilbert," I know the unfortunate incident with Mr. George did not matter, because clearly, I am smart enough to be a doctor, and a damn good one. Because of the words and actions of affirmation from my parents and other supporters, I picked myself up and kept it moving — even if the statement would become a trigger anytime I had any doubts or smaller incidents that reminded me of that special day with the future Dr. Keith Amos.

It was not long before Keith Amos achieved the feat of adding "impressive and promising physician" to his title card. When he graduated from Harvard Medical School, he completed his surgical residency at Washington University in St. Louis and went on to earn a surgical oncology fellowship at MD Anderson Cancer Center in Houston. Dr. Amos served throughout the North Carolina area, and his stellar career culminated in Edinburgh, Scotland.[2] Hailing from our city in Louisiana, Dr. Keith Amos brought us a great sense of pride. He was a strong inspiration to all of us younger than him who had an opportunity to meet or know about him, what could be possible for our own lives if we kept our eyes on the ball. In that moment with my high school chemistry teacher, Mr. George, I experienced a two-fold event: I was able to see a glimpse of my own future through Keith Amos, and I got a dose of what it feels like to have someone try to quell a dream. Fortunately for me, the influence that weighed the most was that of Dr. Amos.

Now that I have my full footing in medicine and a blooming family, I wonder what it would have felt like to connect with Dr. Amos and thank him for serving as a guiding light in my life. I imagine I would schedule an appointment for lunch, fly to wherever he was, and over a meal share with him my story, expressing gratitude for him being himself and taking time to reach back. I imagined his response — a mixture of modesty coupled with pride just as he presented to my high school chemistry class all those years ago about the fact that I traveled to him simply to tell him "Thank you" over lunch. He learned the art of giving back before he crossed the finish line. Even before he had his own diploma in hand, he wanted to get kids from his city ignited right away. Keith was not obligated to return to his high school alma mater to talk to our class. There are lots of people who feel no responsibility for paying their blessings forward with the intention to inspire someone else. That small act of kindness by Harvard Medical School student, Keith Amos, changed my life. Maya Angelou once told Oprah Winfrey that she had no idea what her legacy would be because someone's legacy is every human being they touch and affect in a positive way. I am proud to say I am part of the legacy of Dr. Keith Amos.

I am sad I will never have the chance to act on my desire to pay Dr. Amos a visit. I learned through an eloquent and heart-felt biography written about him by his now widow, that in 2013, he died suddenly due to an acute aortic dissection, a tear in the inner layer of his aorta, during his trip as a visiting scholar in Edinburgh, Scotland. At that time, Dr. Amos had full footing as a physician and a beautiful family of his own.

Dr. Keith Amos died in honor and in service to our world, showing us that it is not how long we live that is most important, but how we choose to live our lives with the time we are given.

Regardless of what anyone tells you that is intended to take away from who you are and what you believe you were put on this earth to contribute, don't listen to them. Oftentimes, people who act this way are unsure of their own life's purpose and wish to throw you off your more certain one. Do not heed their words. Look to whoever you know believes in you — this person or people might be mom, dad, or some other family member. It could be a coach, teacher, pastor, or a summer camp instructor. A core believer in you might even come in the form of a friend or colleague. Or you can pull from the positive energy of someone that you have never met but only read about or saw on TV. Pull from that source of inspiration and allow it to help you wade through the muddy waters of negativity and bring you back to shore so you can continue your journey to your own success.

What I learned from my experience in high school was the inclination to never put someone else through that same hurt while they are trying to do their best to succeed. Even now, there are countless times when I engage with someone who is not as far along as I am, and because I see my previous self in them, I am determined not to let them fall, just as others have done for me. I know this journey to becoming a medical professional and as it is ongoing, so will support need to be. The coast is never clear in my line of work. There are moments where I get to exhale and reflect for a brief amount of time, but as a physician, I am always striving to be better. There is always new technology, a new technique, a new medicine, a new find, a new study — something that can improve the way we as physicians and scientists can help improve mankind.

When I encounter students who are nervous about their next part of the journey, apprehensive about whether or not they will achieve a competitive score on the Medical College Admissions Test (MCAT) or be able to endure the many years required to become a physician, I tell them, "You can get there. Some parts of it might be more challenging than others, but you can get there." For the most part, they do. I know that even in the vast world of medicine, our paths are not always a straight road. Some of us travel straight from undergraduate school to medical school and then on to residency. Then there are some of us who earn another degree after college before going on to medical school, like I did. Some of us had to pause after undergraduate school and work to get our finances together to be able to afford attending medical school. Some of us already have a family started while grinding through medical school or residency. One way or another, we toil, and we get there. Silence the doubt, and so will you.

R.I.P. Dr. Keith Amos. Long live your legacy and its imprint on the future.

3

HBCU Pride

"Education's purpose is to replace an empty mind with an open one."
- Malcolm Forbes

D espite the lingering anxiety that it may have caused me, I thank God for my experience with Mr. George in high school. Until then, I had not experienced any real adversity from the outside world, and I needed an opportunity to figure out how to fall and get back on my feet in a real way before I left my family nest.

College challenges pose a different level of difficulty because the entire experience, for the most part, is one created by choices you make versus choices being made for you by parents or other guides. A key example is that in high school, most of my academic courses were already laid out via the school curriculum. In college, while there is an overall theme to follow to fulfill requirements for a degree, there are dozens of courses from which to choose that all point to the same goal. Even with support from a personal advisor, one can choose an off-beam class for various reasons. Either the requirement for this class will be too difficult or stressful for the rest of the academic load chosen, it does not fulfill the expectation of what was first assumed, or for some other reason is unfavorable. Whatever the rationale, pulling out of a college course once you decide you no longer wish to take it is often not as easy as it seems. Even if you manage to pick the "right" courses, what happens if you choose the "wrong" major? "Wrong" meaning either choosing one that has minimal potential to help you achieve your ultimate dream, or during your college experience, you decide you no longer want to pursue the career your current track was based on. Making a wrong choice can lead to serious repercussions, and these are just two of the many facets of how a college experience can be daunting.

With my GPA and the well-roundedness that most of my previous teachers celebrated about me, I had a solid variety of colleges to choose from. My athletic skills would have earned me certain scholarships at a greater number of schools, but I had a set idea for what kind of school I wanted to attend. Three key factors shaped my final decision. First, after several years of playing a list of varsity sports, as well as spending summers serving as a dedicated teammate in AAU basketball, I decided to hang up my shoelaces and not play college basketball. I was a strong, dependable, and successful athlete, but not one who had a burning desire or was on track to play in the WNBA or any other professional sport, so I let that chapter close for me on a high note in high school. Second, I wanted to remain in the South, particularly in Louisiana, but I cut out colleges like Louisiana State University (LSU) or Baylor University in Texas because, three, I also knew I wanted to attend an HBCU (Historically Black Colleges and Universities). Many of my greatest supporters attended HBCUs: my father, once a standout football player at his alma mater, Jackson State University (Mississippi); my mother, a distinguished graduate of Alcorn State University (Mississippi); my sister, a proud graduate of Talladega College (Alabama) and Southern University Law School (Louisiana); as well as many of my parents' friends and our extended family. There was a sense of pride I felt growing up through their collective spirit whenever there were large HBCU gatherings to attend. Just as much as some children want to follow in the footsteps of mom, dad, aunt, or grandfather to Harvard, Yale, Princeton, or Stanford, I wanted to follow in the steps of my personal heroes and attend an HBCU. I could not wait for the chance.

I mentioned earlier that the adversities of college many times stem from the choices young adults get to make as a sign of newfound independence. I put myself in an interesting situation. Regardless of the triggering, negative comment made by my science teacher, in my head and heart I was still keen on medical school, perhaps even more so with his potentially paralyzing doubt fluttering around me. If Keith Amos could attend medical school, so could I. However, Harvard Medical School student Keith, also a believer in HBCU education, took a tried-and-true route to get there. He attended Xavier University in New Orleans, Louisiana, an HBCU well-known for preparing Black students for medical school. Legions of Black doctors, especially from the South, will count their Xavier undergraduate experience as fertile training ground for a pre-med student. The school is well known for its credible pre-med professors, and the program itself is extremely strong. I would imagine when a student first arrives at Xavier and expresses an interest in medicine, faculty come running from all corners of the campus to offer advice and guide them along the narrow road to get to and through medical school. Nevertheless, I did not choose Xavier. Instead I chose a "cool" school known for some areas of academics but also its share of parties. It was considered the largest HBCU in the country at the time: Southern University in Baton Rouge, Louisiana. With Southern, or "SU," I did not choose the straight path to medical school. However, in the mainstream world, every HBCU is often considered a variant of the same.

After all, it has been well understood throughout history and even today in barbed writings, whispers, and straight-up gossip, how much less regarded are HBCUs versus Predominately White Institutions (PWIs). The mainstream world, popular culture, or basically, "White culture," has deemed an education from an HBCU less prominent than schools with mostly White students. Systematically, PWIs have better resources, higher endowments, and therefore higher scholarships, higher credentialed professors, better housing, and the list of considered "betters" go on and on. For those of us who complete our undergraduate journeys at an HBCU, it is an empowering feeling to cross a stage during graduation as a Black person and look out at a sea of people who look like you and who are as committed to your education as you are. Everything is familiar and supportive. We know it will be one of the last times where almost everyone around us will support and want us to win – just because. Schools like Howard, Morehouse, Spelman, and Xavier may have more of a "brainy" reputation than Southern, but they will always belong to the same cookout. And no matter where we end up — be it moving on to a mainstream graduate school or a global working position — being a part of the HBCU community will forever be special.

Still, I had to choose a school that was considered more "fun," where it seemed that every Black college student (and not) in the southeast would flock to our weekend parties, as my training ground for medical school. Not playing sports in college gave new freedom and time while adjusting to all the other things that

So... When Do I See the Doctor?

come with being away from home for the first time. With no teachers telling me exactly what I was going to do for academics, and no parent or coach to tell me how to spend my non-practice time, my social life quickly filled this position. I gravitated to a crowd of like-minded and fashion-conscious schoolmates who had similar academic values as me but were more familiar with the social scene. I had spent most of my afterschool time in high school playing sports or doing chores at home. In college, it became a priority to shop for new clothes and put extra effort into my physical appearance. Not for a boyfriend, but because it was the culture of the school. At HBCUs, it is not normal for students to be seen loafing around campus wearing their dad's old sweatpants and the same T-shirt four days in a row. My group of friends might have been more the studious type, but like everyone else surrounding us, we still looked stylish. All day. Everyday. Maybe at other schools, students might not care as much about their outward presentation, but at Southern, it was not an option. During my former years under the thumb of my parents and everyone else who served as my village, I watched first-hand how to work hard and play hard so there was rarely a concern about whether I was going to let any form of outside influence divert my eye off the ball. Remember, I was groomed as both an academic and as an athlete — specifically a defensive one. I was trained to respond in the right way to challenges. It was my job to manage many moving parts on a court, having so many variables and angles to consider before I made a move. So surely deciding when to retreat from the Yard and go back to my room to study was not a problem that I would allow myself to have. Though there was so much more to do other than schoolwork at SU, I was determined to keep my young life focused and in balance.

I was immersed in an environment where everyone looked like me to some extent — a first — and it felt incredible. My high school had many Black students, but it was still considered "predominantly White." And, despite my parents intentionally surrounding me with adults who identified as Black, all with different skills, specialties, and vocations, they still taught me that the world at large had a different depiction of my people. In the movies, we were often characterized as lazy, irresponsible, violent, and without vision. Often, cinematics showed young Black boys as anxious with limited or no outlets, driven to destructive lives. Young Black girls were shown having babies before graduating high school, many times dropping out before getting their diplomas. It was like a trap for many youths to predominantly see or hear these portrayals of us. It felt like they were engraining, "Give them as little as possible to hope for or believe in, then watch how they, one by one, lose their footing and end up adding to their own demise." I watched my father throughout my childhood and early adulthood try to pull as many of these young boys and girls from the edge as he could.

In my mind, I had to choose an HBCU, where Black people were infused with a communal feeling of empowerment. Everywhere you looked, even on the Yard, young Black people were searching and doing, putting forth positive efforts to find their purpose in life. Even if some of them did not make it across the finish line (or however long it took them to get there), Lord knows they at least tried. At that time in my life, it was extremely important for me to not be the minority in the room, to feel a sense of emotional ease. It was beneficial for me to be able to spread my wings socially and also put my academic acumen to work in an environment where I did not have to experience the day-to-day anxiety of wondering if the color of my skin was going to prevent me from the level of excellence I deserved. At Southern University, I could truly be Kimberly Gilbert, a young woman who was on a mission to earn her way to becoming a doctor, her way.

As peculiar as it seemed for me to have chosen Southern as my path to medical school, it was revealed to me sooner than later that my gut instincts were for the win although it was not without trial.

Everything about my college choice was off beat for what I hoped to achieve for my career path, including how I became a student at the university. For starters, a pre-med student would perhaps have had their final decision in mind months, maybe even years, before they sought to attend a certain school. I decided two weeks before my first year of college to attend Southern and had the nerve to apply for a coveted Honors College spot, which I was told were filled. A valuable tool I learned from my parents is being able to conduct myself respectfully and be informed. This trait earned me a position of being taken seriously when, albeit late, I appealed to Dean Beverly Wade, who helmed the Honors College at the time. Using my honesty, humility, passion, and knowledge about Southern University, I expressed to her my eagerness to attend her college and my commitment to excellence. So impressed by my proposal, a place was "found" for me in the Honors College, including an academic scholarship and a room in the coveted Honors Dormitory. The Honors college was known for regular meetings with students, ensuring no student lagged. If by chance an Honors College student's grades began to decline, there would be an intentional effort made by the faculty to help bring that student back up to speed. I knew this would serve me along my journey. While I did not exactly have a wavering mind, it was a comforting feeling knowing there was wisdom in the midst that was unwilling to let me fail. It felt like home.

A long my journey, I can remember the time approaching to take the MCAT. I had done well in all my science, math, and literature courses as well as spent each summer participating in science programs at Purdue, Dartmouth, and others, so I believed I could study for the test with my own study plan and pass. I was not daunted that Southern did not have a strong traditional pre-med program. Knowing this, I chose to major in Microbiology to give me even more post-college options. My entire experience thus far was one of hard work and extraordinary blessings, so I felt my MCAT process would be the same.

While I know students often enroll in test preparatory courses to prepare for standardized exams like the MCAT, I also knew how diligent I could be on my own. Because many of these courses tend to be very expensive, it was also important to me not to impose any financial burden on my parents to provide me with test prep course money. I bought several used, popular MCAT preparation books from the nearby LSU campus bookstore and put myself to work. I created a solid study schedule and stuck to it, making it priority over any party or other social activity. When it was time to sit down and fill in ovals on the pages, I felt ready. While I believed in myself and was confident in my test perfor-mance, I lacked real guidance on my process for preparation. Therefore, when the results came back, I should not have been surprised. My score was not a competitive one.

My professor ally throughout this process was a doctor, though not one of medicine. His name was Dr. Bryan Lewis, a

PhD. We were aligned in perspective with the idea of not considering obstacles a permanent impediment but more an opportunity to surmount them. With me and all my classmates, Dr. Bryan Lewis was the epitome of an educator. He achieved the great feat of speaking in a language that students could understand and appreciate for them to embrace the information he taught, knowing it would help them excel. Everyone loved him, including me. He knew that his scope of knowledge could not get me to the soaring finish line of the MCAT, but he was an incredible encourager along the way. Unlike Mr. George in high school, the moment I shared with Dr. Lewis my desire to become a doctor, he was fully on board, offering affirming words like, "Kimberly, everyone's path is different even if it's ultimately getting to the same place. You will be a doctor one day! Just follow the path marked out for you." Failure was not an option with him. He reminded me that it was only a matter of time, and one more solid try using the first shot at the exam as a learning opportunity, and I would win. His words were often prophetic. At the right time, I did.

Despite not having that fertile pre-medical school training, my knowledge and ability to overcome obstacles grew stronger. Also, a sense of heightened community with purpose was harnessed at Southern when a second experience happened and helped shape the kind of person I knew I was destined to be: pledging to serve in the phenomenal Delta Sigma Theta Sorority, Incorporated.

Knowing I am Delta today has me smiling with a confidence that spans more than my own generation. My mother and Aunt Tru pledged Delta, and I grew up watching them don their gorgeous crimson and cream often. I relished hearing about how honorable it was being a part of the sisterhood, and I lived vicariously through their excitement, watching as they prepared for events or service projects their chapter was hosting. With the same intensity that I wanted to become a doctor I also knew I wanted to be one who was service driven in a community sense. Pledging Delta helped me achieve that goal and becoming a Soror was a dream come true.

Many young African American students long to become one of the "Divine Nine," to be a part of a sorority or fraternity that is committed to the advancement of African American people as well as do their part to make the world better overall. And, yes, it looks good to put on a resume, to wear the paraphernalia, and connect with other members of the D9 family. But, to become a part of any Greek organization, there is a rigorous and exhausting process, and someone who is faint of heart should not apply. I knew that earning the status of "Devastating Diva," even if I would be considered a legacy, would not be an easy feat.

Delta Sigma Theta Sorority, Incorporated was founded in 1913 by Black female Howard University students whose intention was to create an exclusive community of educated women who focused on public service, specifically within the African American demographic. Today, the illustrious sorority holds over 200,000 members around the globe. The membership is comprised of various women in leadership — from corporate, educational, social, political, medicine, law, arts, and entertainment. Some of the notable members of Delta Sigma Theta Sorority Incorporated are Dr. Alexa Canady, who at age twenty-six became our nation's first Black neurosurgeon; Shirley Chisolm, the first African-American to run for any major party's United States presidential nomination, and the first female to run for the Democratic Party's presidential nomination award-winning journalist, Soledad O'Brien; acclaimed writer and poet, Dr. Nikki Giovanni; Barbara Jordan, the first Black female elected to the Texas Senate; and civil rights leader, Dorothy Height. There are many highly visible faces of entertainment who proudly wear our signature crimson and cream such as beloved television and movie stars Lena Horne and Angela Bassett, and "living legend" actress Cicely Tyson. Many of our most talented singers, including Shirley Caesar, Roberta Flack, as well as our world's Queen of Soul, Aretha Franklin, I get to proudly call fellow Soror.[3]

Going through the pledging journey to become part of Delta Sigma Theta Sorority, Incorporated was more than a gift. For starters, I learned to appreciate a different level of sisterhood outside the precious one I was born into with Ericka. I became an even better student, woman, and human being because of my affiliation. I began to understand the selfless commitment to serving others no matter who they are, and this philosophy would carry over into my profession of medicine. There is nothing I have done on a professional or personal level that has not been supported by a fellow Soror. Regardless of the field in which we are climbing, if there is another Delta in the place, you can rest assured there will be wisdom and support to spare. I am most grateful to the two women who first introduced me to the wonders of the organization: Mom and Aunt Tru.

By the time I became a senior at SU, I had experienced the many attributes and the few setbacks of choosing Southern University to serve as the foundation for my journey to becoming a physician. I adjusted to life not filled with sports and worked my way around the lack of sound pre-medical preparation, which contributed to me not faring as well as I would have liked on the MCAT. Finally, I learned how to balance academic pressure with social and community avocation and activism. Despite any adversity I had during college, I would not change any of it. My experience at Southern did what it was supposed to do: It taught me how to make wise choices when no one is watching.

My newly earned wisdom made me aware that graduating with great grades, yet a not-so-competitive MCAT score, was not going to land me in my ideal medical school. Therefore, I chose another nontraditional route (yes, again) to build my science knowledge and to learn how to quickly internalize and understand greater amounts of information to be better prepared to take the MCAT the next time. Soon after graduating from Southern, I enrolled in a Master of Science program in Indianapolis, Indiana. I knew I had to focus intensely, and, coupled with an extreme region shift from the South to the Midwest, the master's program served its purpose as a steady bridge but not my destination.

Up until then, I was mostly on my own regarding my road to medical school. The master's program in Indianapolis added focus into my life, as well as a new equally focused friend named Candace who rode that wave with me. We were both pursuing our rightful places into the medical world in the chilly city of Indianapolis. Candace and I were kept warm by our after-class study sessions at the nearby Chinese buffet, quizzing each other over sesame chicken and sautéed string beans. We had so much in common, having attended an HBCU (she was a Florida A&M University graduate) and she was also a Soror. She was a no-nonsense woman like I was, and she was a perfect blend of brains, style, athleticism, and beauty. Candace was my ace then and continues to be to this day.

So... When Do I See the Doctor?

The saying is true about focus and hard work: They do pay off. Two years after I had mastered the art of warming up my car in advance during the frigid winter months, I emerged from the Master of Science program with a new master's degree, a new competitive MCAT score that was key to my acceptance into my top choice of medical schools, along with a new attitude.

4

The Trenches

"Smooth seas do not make skillful sailors."
- African Proverb

resh from the Midwest and back in Louisiana, I returned ready for my new life at Louisiana State University (LSU) Medical School in New Orleans, Louisiana. What a joy to be back home, so close to my family again. My parents and surrounding village were proud I had completed the master's program. I was proud of myself as well. I felt jubilant to have "brought it all back home" so to speak. I felt prepared for my next chapter, though my first year was tough but promising.

That first Monday, one of the well-meaning upperclassmen came to a group of us and said, "Let me help you understand the level of how you better learn fast and learn it right the first time." He pointed to a mountain of his class notes that could have been nicknamed Everest and said, "You have until Friday to learn all of this." I must admit, the conversation in my inner monologue started with, "Oh shit!" I thought about what would happen if my dad was observing from the sidelines and I looked at him after being presented with a comparable physical challenge. He would mouth to me, "You got this." And like all the other moments when he said it, he was right. I did. I zeroed in on the towering stack of notes with determined eyes, undaunted with a focused glare ready to accept this latest challenge. I channeled two of our world's greatest athletes, Muhammed Ali, and Michael Jordan, and embodied their "game on" persona. Pinch me. I, Kimberly Gilbert, had successfully completed undergraduate studies, a master's program, and I was now embarking on my first year of medical school.

I was managing medical school the same way I managed the basketball court as a point guard, knowing when to press and when to slow play so the game stayed in my control. I learned how to process hundreds of papers weekly. I was fine-tuning my way of taking notes and understanding information for success on exams. No question, I entered LSU with an intention to win, and nothing less.

Proud of myself is a phrase I would use, but I am not sure if it fully explains my feelings. Think about anything you worked years to achieve, sometimes met with success, but other times, met with some degree of failure or a derailment that you have a split second to decide which way to go next. No matter what, you keep going. Imagine toiling through challenge after challenge, and finally you begin to see a light in the clearing. The more you grind, the brighter the light gets. And then, after such a long time maintaining focus, the representation of the bright light is awarded to you in a form of your opportunity to now show all that you have learned, putting you that much closer to the greater goal, whatever that goal is for you. Is it pride that you feel? Relief? Joy? Triumph? My greater goal was to become a doctor, and serving as a physician today, I can share that earning the position in medicine is an awesome thing. However, there is something about the moment when a student enters medical school that compares to nothing else. If being a physician is the Big League, medical school is the coveted draft and training camp to get you there.

During my first year of medical school, I was running on a mix of adrenaline, knowledge, and a belief in myself to reinforce the truth that making it this far only meant I was destined to prevail. That first year gave me a full handle on the lay of the land, which was somewhat less challenging to accomplish because I had returned to an environment with which I was familiar. Upon crossing that first-year finish line, I exhaled a brief sigh of relief all while looking forward to the continued possibilities ahead. This milestone also brought on a sense of sobriety because it was reported that two of my schoolmates had committed suicide by the end of the school year, succumbing to the immense pressure often placed upon medical students, whether it be from family, friends, professors, or themselves. It is a tragic reminder that sometimes we never know what people are struggling with and how hopeless it seems in their minds. I looked back wondering, "What did I not see? Should I have stopped longer to talk?" I may never know what, if anything, may have made a difference in those situations. But it opened my eyes to understand the importance of mental health and trying to recognize when someone may be expressing a "cry for help".

With respect to classes, I entered my second year with relative ease, brushing the dust off my shoulders and feeling even more confident about all the information I had retained the year before. I wiped my brow and was eager to enter Round Two. By then, I had galvanized a group of friends, or shall I say, a "committee" of classmates who were committed to win and help one another along the way. There were four of us: MacArthur Baker, Gersh Norfleet, Kerry Sterling, and me. We studied together, laughed together, and sometimes, helped keep one another awake. I had quickly grown to admire each one of my new friends, and they showed right away how much they had my back. With my medical school village blossoming, though grueling at times, it had become a home away from home.

In hindsight, I believe God set up such a supportive, consistent, and stable environment ahead of time so I would have a safe place to land upon getting a call from my sister and hearing news for which I could have never been prepared. My greatest champion and coach, my nucleus, had been called Home. My daddy had died suddenly of an acute myocardial infarction, also known as a heart attack. The date was July 22, 2002. I was twenty-four years old, and two weeks into my second year of medical school. I was standing in the clearing with a plain-as-day, luminous path ahead, charged, and full of purpose and promise. In an instant, the lights dimmed and began to swirl around me. I tried to remain upright, but the dizzying lights made me lose my balance. My daddy was gone. I was shattered.

Right away, I met with my Dean, who sincerely offered me an opportunity to take the remainder of the year off. Without hesitation, I declined, because I did not want to feel like I was giving up. I thought back to when I was having a bad game and my dad could see the normal brazenness fade from my eyes. He had an uncanny way of helping me see the bigger picture again so I could summon enough energy and drive to see the goal through. Medical school was my big goal in this moment, but in my heart, I had one knee on the ground. It was so hard to get up, but I was committed to not quitting. I tried with everything in me to push my mind and body to work on sheer determination alone. It was hard.

I chose not to take a break from medical school, although the most emotionally traumatic experience to date had happened right in the middle of it. It also was no secret that the second year of medical school was often considered the most difficult. All I could think about was the fact that I would never see Daddy alive again.

I persevered through the pain. I could hear my dad in my ear explaining why I should not give up. My mother and sister did their best to support and encourage me while grieving in their own ways, and Lord knows I also tried to be there for them as best I could. What was left of our Gilbert household were the three women. My mother, our matriarch, had always set a tone of prioritizing family. For me, though, my connection had to be from afar if I planned to continue medical school, even if I would rather have retreated to my childhood bed and imagined Daddy walking down the hall serenading Al Jarreau's "Mornin' Mr. Radio."

I remained in school, but the year went on without me. I traveled through it submerged in a complete fog. I might have verbally committed to my Dean to continue, but success in medical school was based on attendance and performance. Again, I give glory to God for the previous setup of the familiar environment and supportive friends because if it were not for The Committee, I do not know how I would have gotten through that year.

On the many, many days when I felt I was going through the motions, The Committee made sure I still came to the study area we liked to use after class. Often, I would be in a daze and look up from a book only to meet the eyes of Mac, who seemed to be monitoring me all while handling his own business. He would offer a smile to ensure that I was okay. He would ask if I needed to talk then help me to refocus my thoughts. On days when we were not all studying together, he also called me to make sure I knew I was not alone. He wasn't pushy, and all of The Committee allowed me to move at my own pace. This freedom to grieve and go through my process of loss the best way I knew how was invaluable to me. Without them, my mom and sister, and most important, God, there is no way I could have finished that year, let alone two more years still waiting for their turn at me.

Without Daddy's physical presence, there were times when I was tempted by thoughts not so resilient, like triggers from that haunting moment with Mr. George, beckoning me to question my abilities as doctor-to-be. I could not consult with my dad in person or over the phone so I would conjure him up by a voice in my head that would remind me who I was to get myself back on track. Little by little, I had to remember what he had taught me to be true to deal with whatever I was going through. My mom would always shine for me, reminding me who and *whose* I was. Yet, I was groomed by them both, together. They both had their special roles in my life and had specific ways in which they helped push me along. The spirit of my dad was strong, and I knew this was the time when I would have to become even more resilient and self-reliant.

My journey through that year of grief is one that I will never forget. By the time I completed that second chapter of medical school, I had gained even more knowledge, wisdom, and under-standing about my chosen profession as well as my purpose. I was heading toward my final years of medical school, stronger, more humbled, more grateful, and even more sure of myself and what I believe I was brought into the world to do. All of this, and I was also given the blessing of having my daddy, my newest angel that I could call by name, with me all the time.

I emerged from the second, monumental year of medical school, ready to show all that I had learned and put my knowledge to action. The first two years of medical school were more classroom-based. The second half which includes wearing a lab coat, albeit short, takes things to another level.

B y year three, I was showing such aptitude that I was accepted into a summer program for students interested in the specialty of orthopedics. This acceptance gave me a greater sense of confidence because it was uncommon that female medical students even pursued, much less got accepted into, anything relating to orthopedics.[4]

Ultimately, I chose to pursue Physical Medicine & Rehabilitation (PM&R) and, during my fourth year, applied to a PM&R residency program because the discipline spoke to me on both a professional and spiritual level. I knew I wanted to become a physician because helping people is what I have seen all my life and what I enjoy doing. I believe PM&R is a special kind of medicine. Every day, to be trained with the knowledge and skill to formulate comprehensive medical treatment plans while also having the personality to "coach people up" to achieve physical feats as complex as regaining the strength and coordination to return their bodies to the level required to compete in a professional sport, all the way to the other end of the spectrum where my training is key to helping patients achieve the most precious acts such as lifting a finger again after their body has been ravaged by a stroke, woke me up with a heightened purpose. I understand that the skill is science, but I also believe a component of healing is spiritual.

There are countless times when science can report a supposed impossibility of a physical feat for a patient, and most times there is some truth to the data. However, there is something that compliments science, called sheer will, that can take someone over the most seemingly impossible hurdles even science cannot explain. My dad was the finest coach I knew, and I observed him create game plans and encourage players every day to achieve what they at first thought was impossible. My dad was an excellent role model for me and adding that skill set to my level of scientific expertise later became my penchant of sorts in the field. Life is never black and white. Sometimes, all we need to do is BELIEVE.

Upon graduation, I was on the most incredible high. The light in the clearing was bold and bright; I could see straight ahead. With my mother and sister in the audience, clapping with tears in their eyes, I felt a sense of fulfillment and honor. I had done what I set out to do. Through Southern University, the Master of Science program in Indianapolis, and then getting through the passing on of my dad, I had done it; just as he and my mom both said I would. I had become a physician. And I did it in the way that was sculpted for me. I walked down the stairs of the stage with my diploma in my hands and whispered to the Heavens, "Daddy, I got this."

5

The Ancestors

"Pass the truth to the next generation. Teach them early what we learn late."
- Unknown

A long my journey to and through residency, I experienced a share of encounters with my fellow Black/African American people on both sides of this field.

Helping patients who suffered from medical conditions that were disproportionately detected in Black people gave me a stronger sense of purpose for where I was headed.

Engaging with other Black physicians along the way brought on an even greater sense of pride. The road that led to becoming a doctor was indeed my own, yet it was also one that in many ways is shared by other Black physicians in the spirit of feeling the need to work three times as hard as everyone else. As a Black physician in any specialty, we know that in the vast field of medicine we will encounter our share of discrimination and second-guessing of our skills just because of how we look. We also have in the back of our minds that despite having the same, or sometimes more, knowledge than our White counterparts, we will at times have to fight for equal recognition and compensation for the hard work we do.

Since Western medicine became more popular in America in the early 19th century, Black people, both as practitioners and as patients, have had a complicated, and sometimes tragic, relationship with it.

I am paying tribute to those like Sara "Saartjie" Baartman (Hottentot Venus), Henrietta Lacks, and the 600 male subjects of the cruel Tuskegee syphilis experiment that began in 1932. To the countless numbers of enslaved Black women who endured the subhuman, and many times lethal, treatment at the hands of who America deemed the "father of modern gynecology," James Marion Sims [5]: I speak and bless your names. All these Black people were subjected to some form of inhumane act for the sake of advancing medicine for the western world. Our Black bodies, not viewed as precious, were ripped, burned, cut, poisoned, and TERRORIZED. Black people were tortured and sundered to provide White physicians with ways to create solutions for the health advancement of WHITE people. The means to the ends were not always as straightforward. Sometimes, the devious deeds were accomplished through deception.

The Black males who were the subjects of the Tuskegee experiment agreed to participate because they were told that they would receive free healthcare from the federal government of the United States.[6]

Henrietta Lacks had no idea that her extraordinary "HeLa" cells collected by her physician after being treated for cervical cancer would be used to push forward science and lead to a world-renowned medical breakthrough in the 1950s. Ms. Lacks died without compensation for her invaluable yet involuntary contribution.[7]

In the early 19th century, South African Sara "Saartjie" Baartman was repeatedly exploited due to her physical appearance for immediate monetary gain and scientific study. After her death, Ms. Baartman's remains were not initially put to rest, as scientists and profiteers had her body dissected and analyzed in an attempt to prove false theories about Black people's correlation to animals. It was not until later when then South African President Nelson Mandela formally requested the return of her remains that her body was finally laid to rest in 2002.[8]

Modern day medicine was built on the bodies of wailing in pain, enslaved African men and women who were brutally sacrificed time and time again during a litany of experimental procedures.

Knowing that the African American person's historical relationship with medicine was often wrought with terror and fear, and knowing that even today there are various medical injustices committed against Black and Brown people, I vowed to be the continuous change I wanted to see in the world of medicine as I approached my opportunity to perform as a physician full-time.

On the other side of the field, choosing to serve as a physician is not always a "straight line to the finish line" when you are of color. Many Black and Brown physicians will more often admit that their road to earning a white coat and the letters "MD", "DO", or "DPM" after their name did not happen in an "American Dream" sort of way.

For starters, to become a medical doctor, there is a great deal that must be sacrificed for a period of time, and socio-economically, many Black and Brown students bear too much of a financial load to put their lives on hold and pursue medicine. Black people who earn college degrees hope to generate income soon after the diploma is in hand. In addition to keeping their own lives afloat, there might be other family members a young Black college student may feel responsible to financially contribute to. If there is no level of financial stability around, it can feel near impossible to see through to a vision of practicing medicine that begins with four years of college, four years of medical school, and three-plus years of residency. My road took an extra two years because remember, I also earned a Master of Science degree prior to attending medical school. Ultimately, the journey to crossing the finish line to medicine can take eleven years or more after high school, which to some can seem insurmountable.

The road to becoming a physician is much longer than many other coveted degrees, and physician hopefuls need some-thing to help them survive along the way because to be success-ful, we must be one hundred percent "all in." Medical school is nothing like undergraduate studies. Once you have been accept-ed, your level of focus must be high — each year more so than the next. There are times when you might become discouraged because your friends who entered the workforce right after college seem to be making money and having more time for fun. You, too, can overall enjoy your life in medical school but not in the same way as your friends. My level of discipline has always been strong, and so almost like a light switch, I could turn the fun off and on.

So... When Do I See the Doctor?

The process of earning your medical stripes is grueling in and of itself, and if there are outside pressures — that is, any other responsibilities that demand your time such as having to help care for a family — there must be an understanding that your ability to be present may sometimes be limited. I know people who had small children and were able to get through medical school because they had amazing, supportive partners or parents who were willing and able to take the lead during their children's early years. If you are blessed with something as precious as a family while you are in medical school, in order to keep a healthy balance of your time, quality over quantity must be the theme of the day where you are concerned. Everything must be intentional. I have witnessed many times "smart" people with good intentions fail to make it to the finish line because they didn't realize or understand just how much discipline is needed to complete medical school. So many people — Black, White, and others — throw in the towel because they feel the pressure is too much. The academic pressure is too much. The financial pressure is too much. And it is just too hard to focus with those issues plus the other life responsibilities that can place ultimatums on you.

Before you even walk into the medical school or residency program you desire to attend, you are expected to venture out to the schools or programs for the purpose of an in-person interview. You must wear the "right" outfit to each interview, and for each of these interviews, you must provide for your own travel and lodging. I skirted some of that financial burden by keeping my search limited to a certain region then scheduling my interviews where I could pay less airfare for a "multi-leg" flight for places too far to drive. In cities where I had family, I stayed with them for the night.

With a few good suits that I recycled along the way, I was able to get to many of the interviews offered to me.

The adversities I speak of have primarily to do with economics, and the heavy imbalance of economics and overall wealth distribution stems in part from racism. Why is it so many intellectually capable Black students who have dreams to attend medical school never do? Because the dream itself feels unrealistic and inconceivable? It is because the process to become a doctor is a costly endeavor, and with Black people still only receiving a small slice of this great American pie, the average Black family does not have the finances set aside to help their child or children get to and through medical school. This holds true even with a student loan — which by the way is notorious for also leaving you with a sometimes lifelong, mortgage-size monthly payment after graduation. The same goes for other people of color, like Latin Americans. The saying, "you have to spend money to make money" applies to the ambitious goal of becoming a doctor. You do not have to have a lot of money in the bank to succeed, but someone or something must serve as a sponsor for your cause. Of course, scholarships and other financial aid help a great deal, as well as sympathetic loved ones who are willing to help you remain nourished while you endure the grueling hours of medical school and residency. If you are determined, you can overcome any of these challenges. Having just-enough monetary support behind you, a strong will, and refusal to give up should help get you through.

Even after my dad passed, I knew I had to push forward and not throw in the towel. My father instilled within me a sense of community that whatever I chose to pursue, it was not for me alone. I know my quest to succeed as a doctor was to make not only me, my family, and my future family proud, but it was also for the lives sacrificed on the receiving end of medicine as well as for those before me who cleared the path as best as they could so that African Americans know what is possible. No matter what, I am determined to win. And if this desire is in your heart as much as it is in mine, you can, too.

"Courage is not the absence of fear, but rather the judgement that there is something more important than fear."
-Ambrose Redmoon

Before my and many other African American doctors' own uphill battles initiated, there existed African American medical trailblazers who dared to pursue medicine. Their courage and achievements began to shift not only the landscape of who could legitimately hold a scalpel or wear a stethoscope in the mainstream, but they also opened windows to the medical world to more than just White hopefuls.

Dr. Daniel Hale Williams was one of our great pioneering Black physicians who understood right away that his advancement should be used to pave the way for others. Encyclopedia Britannica affirmed that in 1893, Dr. Williams performed one of the earliest successful open-heart surgeries.[9] But he did not initially seek to pursue medicine. It was the standard of that time for freed Blacks to set their sights on manual labor, so Dr. Williams was encouraged to follow in the footsteps of his father and serve as a barber. During the time he was working at his barbershop in Wisconsin, Dr. Williams became intrigued with the work of a local physician. Soon after he was exposed to the doctor's work, he became fascinated with medicine and began an apprenticeship

under Dr. Henry Palmer before attending Chicago Medical College, which would later be named Northwestern University Medical School. After graduation, he started his own private practice
for patients of all races.

Not intimidated that Black doctors were not allowed to work
in American hospitals, Dr. Williams set out on a path less traveled
and pioneered many things throughout his career. One of his
most significant contributions to medicine was Provident Hospital
in Chicago, the first integrated hospital in the United States, which
he founded in 1891 to provide a platform for himself and other
Black physicians, medical residents, and nurses to practice.
Provident Hospital provided a facility where people in the neigh-
boring communities who needed more access to health care
could receive adequate attention from any of the quality, racially
diverse physicians on his medical team. After successfully providing this balanced system of medical care, Dr. Williams further
opened doors for those African Americans who wanted to enter
the nursing field. He did not stop there. In 1893, he was appointed
surgeon-in-chief of Freedman's Hospital in Washington, D.C. That
same year, he became the first African American on record to
successfully perform surgery on the pericardium (open heart
surgery) without using Penicillin or a blood transfusion, and that
patient lived for twenty more years after having had the procedure
done under Dr. Williams' care. Despite limitations for Black doctors to be a part of a wider medical association, he co-founded the
National Medical Association for African American physicians in
1895. Later in 1913, Dr. Williams was inducted into the American
College of Surgeons as a charter member and its only African
American member.[10]

So... When Do I See the Doctor?

Dr. Williams did not rest on the laurels of his innovative work in surgery. He set out to create a world where people like me could also thrive in the field. Having no mirroring images of himself directly in front of him to inspire him to proceed with his dream, he moved purely on courage alone. The awareness of his existence compels me to move forward and upward, no matter the obstacle. Somehow through time and space, Dr. Williams' entrepreneurial endeavors paved the way for my own business aspirations. My physiatry practice strives to implement many of the key initiatives that mirror Provident Hospital's mission, in that we are inclusive of and equally care for all races and cultures. We also provide for those who do not have the financial means to receive proper rehabilitation care with the same enthusiasm and skill as we do for any other patients. This philosophy also carries over into my Life Care Planning business, which provides people with a detailed "game plan" for their lives after suffering a catastrophic injury or illness. My non-surgical aesthetics practice allows me to combine my fine motor skills and medical expertise with an additional love of "helping people become their most beautiful selves." My "chemistry brain," combined with my love of style and grooming has blessed me to create a hair care line along with my hairstylist, who is also a dear friend. I know in my heart that Dr. Williams' trailblazing made it possible for me to have the thriving medical/scientific entrepreneurial endeavors I have today. He taught me that the possibilities are endless.

While I continue to move forward with my medical career, I am consistently conscious of those who came before me, chopping down the trees of discrimination and cutting through the forests of racism. Dr. Daniel Hale Williams was aware of the limitations around him but did not allow them to hinder his focus on success. He did not weep over a closed door, he created new ones and kept them wide open for more to enter. Dr. Williams did more than protest the racist conditions around him, he maneuvered around those racist conditions and helped change the game.

In the mid-to-late 19th century, few Black doctors existed like Dr. Williams who were bravely initiating new ground for those doctors and nurses who were to follow his lead. There was one physician who decided to take on a literary and educational approach to what legacy she chose to leave behind. Dr. Rebecca Lee Crumpler, the first African American woman to serve as a physician in the United States, proudly practiced medicine for over four decades. Of her numerous contributions spanning her career, Dr. Crumpler authored the heralded, "A Book of Medical Discourses."

Dr. Crumpler was among the women who served as the first admitted female class to the New England Female Medical College. The surrounding community was not supportive, as male physicians vigorously labeled the female medical students as being emotionally unstable and intellectually incapable. The fact that she was a Black woman made her experience even worse. Where her White women counterparts were perhaps belittled, given the era, Dr. Rebecca Lee Crumpler was most likely considered invisible. Still, she pressed on. Graduating in 1864, she began her practice primarily caring for African American women and children. After the Civil War ended, she moved to Richmond, Virginia, and worked for the Freedmen's Bureau to provide medical care for the freed slaves who were denied health care by White doctors. As one of the few Black hires on staff, she was constantly scrutinized and subjected to extreme racism by White colleagues and supervisors. The community of doctors around her refused to validate her position as a medical doctor, and they often committed verbal assaults against her, some even mocking that the "MD" behind her name stood for "Mule Driver."

Dr. Crumpler did not crumble, rather she emerged with a new vision and moved to a more predominantly Black community, choosing to support families who struggled to receive proper care for their children. In 1883, Dr. Crumpler published her ground-breaking " A Book of Medical Discourses," based on the copious notes she had taken throughout her career. In her writings, she offers general medical advice, speaks about health preservation for women and children, and homeopathy, among other relevant topics related to human health and progression. "A Book of Medical Discourses" was the first and only medical book published in the 19th century by a woman, let alone one who was Black.[11]

Dr. Rebecca Lee Crumpler reminds me of parts of my own journey during my professional career in medicine. As a woman, I feel the stings of discrimination, and while I am not happy about the treatment when it happens, the idea of cowering or buckling never comes to mind. I am also not immune to racism. I know it exists, and however subtle or direct, I continue to navigate around its bullets and sabotage. My awareness of Dr. Crumpler's life gives my own even greater meaning. Like Dr. Williams, she was unafraid to keep pushing despite what battles were set before her. She wrote literature to enhance the lives of all people, and at the same time, took time to care for those who looked like her, who were ignored by the medical system because of their race, gender, and not having the means to afford proper healthcare.

Black people were brought to the Americas involuntarily or by deception to be enslaved, working for free to build this country we call the "United" States. After this country was founded and established, The Constitution of The United States affirms many things about "all men's" freedoms — freedoms that do not come easily if your skin looks anything like mine. Part of the freedoms we fight for every day is having the ability to integrate our talents into the world and be recognized for what we have contributed. As much as we contribute to the world at large and integrate into it, the world has an unmistakable way of reminding us at every turn that we are Black and, in their eyes, inferior. Some of us rise higher than others in society through fame and wealth, but in the end, the "biggest society" puts us all in one box. Because of this box we are put in, we as Black people will always have a community feeling among ourselves, even welcoming those Black people who are unwilling to actively claim the community or take part in it. No matter how high we climb, we must never forget those who are left behind or those who paved the way for us to have arrived wherever we stand. To the many ancestral beacons and pillars who, without regret, traversed uncertain roads, and through difficult and oftentimes dangerous circumstances you initiated paradigm shifts for the benefit of all Black people: I honor you, and I am humbly grateful for your sacrifices. I vow to do all I can to help seize the destiny you have left for us to fulfill.

PART TWO

— *THE BRANCHES* —

6

The Road to Residency

"Knowledge is knowing what to say. Wisdom is knowing whether or not to say it."
- Starhawk

B efore starting residency, I had a little time to reflect on my road thus far, reiterate to myself about how much of an accomplishment it already was to be in my current position, and take real time to pay gratitude to God for everything He had done and brought me through. It is wild how a dream can be brought to life — can become REAL. First, by having a dream. Second, by listening to a "Higher Voice" to help guide the forthgoing steps. And third, by taking heed to the "Higher Voice" to get where you are destined to go. Even though I had a plan which I thought was certain, I had to remain open and self-analyze just in case my intent to become a physician had evolved over time. Had my dreams become stronger in one respect or another? Who, if anyone, served as a beacon for my intense drive? Aside from being introduced to then "future doctor" Keith Amos, I had not yet met a physician who I "looked up to" in an extraordinary way. My interest in medicine did not begin with a personal inspiration, rather a love for science after having been introduced and guided by my mother, who taught high school biology and chemistry. Spending time in her classroom while growing up, experimenting with things in the lab, her teaching me many of the wonders of science, became part of my DNA. I believe that the initial idea in my head to pursue medicine after my mom introduced me to the "Operation" game when I was only a little girl was purely organic. Medicine is an extension of science, and for me, those little plastic organ pieces in the game reminded me somewhat of the experiments in my mom's lab. I became more and more fascinated with healing the human body. What most strengthened my determination to get where I stood after having completed medical school was not one particular person, but it had more to do with my overall excitement and passion for helping people.

If my track record of ascension were to remain consistent, of course, there would be some sort of detour to my next leg up. Thus far, I had already chosen a good and, at the same time, "party school" as my pre-med educational foundation. Partly because of this choice, my first go at the MCAT exam was not as high as I would have hoped, so instead of applying to medical school with that score, I instead applied to a Master of Science program to really prepare me for the MCAT my second go-round, which worked out very well. I do not regret any of my choices or the extra schooling because I learned so much during that time. My experience in Indianapolis grew me up in ways that staying close to home would not have. By the time I took the MCAT again after studying with the level of knowledge I acquired while getting my master's degree, I danced out of the test knowing I had won.

I believe that my job was to have a plan but to also remain open to when the Highest Plan was set before me, so I could see what and where I was destined to be. After four years of a challenging, exhausting, at one point very emotional — yet overall fulfilling — experience in medical school, my destiny kept me in

72

Louisiana to complete my internship year at LSU before continuing to Emory for my PM&R residency.

I must admit that at the start of each of my "legs," my spirit was usually at ease. I had yet to stumble into or have a rocky beginning. That chapter in my journey through medicine was no different. Because I had just completed medical school at the same location, I already knew the layout of the campus and the hospital systems. I had built a reputation for being a solid and determined student doctor, and those higher-ups around me were going to receive great pleasure witnessing all that they had instilled in me over the past four years. For me, it was a no brainer to remain in Louisiana for that first year.

My first few weeks into my internship were hitting on all cylinders. Now that I was considered a "resident doctor," and not a "student doctor," my previous sheen of pride elevated to an immense glow. Remaining in Louisiana served beneficial for everyone who remained local because, through colleagues and supervisors, we were all able to witness each other's progression over the years. Knowing the lay of the land also made it helpful, too, because my easy flow was largely made possible by my familiarity with the systems and campus.

As a new resident doctor, at the historic Charity Hospital in New Orleans, a typical day looked like this: I would arrive between 5:30 and 6:00 a.m. to give myself time to see my patients and formulate my SOAP note (subjective, objective, assessment, and plan) before my attending physician arrived around 8:00 a.m. When the attending physician arrives, he or she, along with all the resident doctors and medical students on the team, commence what is called "team rounds" on all patients seen by the resident doctors (and their assigned medical students) that morning. This daily experience provides additional learning for residents because we have an opportunity to learn from each other's patients as well as the attending physician's wisdom and additional recommendations.

After rounding, time would be filled by following up with established patients, checking labs/imaging/other studies, adjusting medications, admitting and managing new patients, and more before signing out that evening. After my shift was over around 5:00 or 6:00 p.m., I would "sign out" to the on-call resident physicians by reviewing each of my patients so they would have a good understanding of each one in case there were any overnight events. Even after doing this I did not rush out just in case a nurse or someone else needed my help. I quickly got the hang of this process, and every three to four days, I was scheduled to be one of the on-call resident doctors, which meant that my 5:30 a.m. start time would not end by 6:00 p.m. Rather, it ended the following morning or early afternoon.

By that third week, I hit my stride even though hurricane season was also in full effect. During hurricane season, winds and heavy rain could be the expected weather of the day, and to walk out of the hospital at the end of a workday and feel the sun kiss my cheeks brought on plenty of reason to rejoice. That Friday, August 26, 2005, was beyond a "Thank God it's..." because I started work in the wee hours on Thursday morning, and by the time I was actually "post-call," I was approaching the "maximum hours allowed" by residency guidelines. So, when the time came, my attending physician gave me "that look," and I high tailed it out of there.

The next day, Mayor Ray Nagin declared a state of emergency and voluntary evacuation of the New Orleans area due the approaching Hurricane Katrina that was scheduled to reach us in the next two to three days (Governor Blanco had declared a state of emergency for the state of Louisiana the day before).[12] I initially thought of driving to my godbrother Dexter's house in Houston to escape the weather, as I usually did when there was a voluntary evacuation issued during hurricane season. It was a four hour drive I had done many times, and I knew Dexter would receive me well. We were practically family, as his mother, Mrs. Hadnot, the entrepreneur who styled much of our neighborhood's hair while growing up, was my godmother. And, since the weather looked relatively fine outside, I figured that I had some time before leaving and would give the people in the lower lying areas of the city time to get a head start.

Over the weekend, though, things started to look more ominous. At one point, the wind started picking up and the rain became heavier with an unfamiliar pattern. At that moment, I changed my mind from going to Dexter's house and decided to brave the shorter, one-hour drive to Baton Rouge and take refuge with Ericka, who lived there at the time.

My parents always stressed the importance of being prepared. "You never know what could happen," was our family's mentality, so I was rarely without a full tank of gas — usually when I saw that my tank was nearing the halfway mark, I would make my way to the gas station to fill it up again. My oil, antifreeze, and any other maintenance that my car needed were always up to date. My tires were kept in good condition. These things, although many others my age might have kept their car upkeep a low priority, were essential to me. I rarely needed to depend on my survival-mode skills, but when I did, I and anyone who was with me was relieved at this character trait. This time though, I was alone, and I was thanking God that me being so particular served me at that moment. With a prayer in head and heart, I took off at the fastest speed the weather would allow, which was at a snail's pace.

From my home, traveling from the New Orleans area to Baton Rouge involved driving over a long bridge, this time seeming to never end. My drive alone was harrowing, as I could not see on either side of me due to the heavy waters crashing down on my car, and the drumming of the downpour was deafening. The combination of wind and rain created a dark sheet that blinded my front view. I could see nothing in front of me — not even the hood of my car. But I kept going. I was terrified driving over the bridge and refused to look around me, thinking I would become paralyzed. "I have to get over this bridge," I continued to direct myself. I kept saying a prayer that I wouldn't somehow drive off of the bridge or crash into anyone. And, driving in such conditions by myself also scared me in another way: If I had to pull over, who would or even could help me?

I did everything that I could to pass the time that would not seem to move fast enough, slowly directing my car whenever the storm's black curtain parted just enough for me to see which way to go. I finally made it over the bridge and was getting closer to my sister's apartment. When I looked at the clock for the umpteenth time, I had been on the road for a grueling nine hours. When I finally pulled into the parking spot, I could have fallen to my knees when I opened the car door. I didn't only because I was in shock. Ericka was so relieved that I made it, and she rushed me inside to safety.

Our lights flickered on and off, sometimes going stretches of hours without power. When we could get a glimpse of what was happening in New Orleans through the news, we could see that it was a disaster. The rain was crashing down with a vengeance. Sitting in my sister's living room in the city of Baton Rouge, that was for sure experiencing much of the same turmoil as New Orleans, I felt so helpless. I can only imagine how I would have handled being sheltered-in-place in Charity hospital.

Over the years, I have spoken with so many colleagues who were trapped at Charity Hospital and other areas during Hurricane Katrina; them pouring out their hearts describing the agony of helplessly having to watch patients die, or them expressing disappointment with how our local and federal governments handled the situation and how unprepared everything and everyone felt. Hearing these stories pierced me within. I might have not been there in Charity Hospital with them, but I had just left there.

I spent my time at Ericka's place doing my best to make sense of my particular ordeal while also dealing with a rollercoaster of emotions about all of my friends and adoptive family that I left behind. Anything could have happened to me during my drive, for there are plenty of stories since the great Hurricane Katrina that speak to fatalities and near-deaths about people who tried to escape the storm as I did.

B y Monday, the levees broke, and all hell broke loose with it. Homes, businesses, landscapes, gone or destroyed beyond repair. People and animals vanished, kidnapped by pilfering winds and water.

I did not have full contact with my colleagues and friends throughout New Orleans to know what was going on and if all were okay. It would be weeks before I heard from them, which was excruciating for me. I had just spent four years of medical school with many of my colleagues and had begun the internship part of my residency, by choice, in New Orleans. I had already secured my full residency at Emory in Atlanta, but I wanted one last year in New Orleans, sort of a bonus year to truly hone my skills before I ended my living experience in Louisiana perhaps for good.

Emory received word that I hadn't gotten trapped in the devastation and proceeded to prepare a way for me to continue my remaining internship there in Atlanta then roll into the remainder of my residency with them as previously planned. A few weeks later, I was offered an opportunity to start at Emory. This was yet another moment of God's saving grace. When I was asked if I could start in a week, I eagerly accepted. "Why wait?" I thought to myself. Even though Atlanta had not experienced a disaster like New Orleans, there were still many people who needed medical attention there for different reasons. But before driving to Atlanta with only the few personal things I decided to grab before evacuating, I needed the full circle opportunity of returning to my neighborhood to see with my own eyes the damage that Hurricane Katrina had done.

Looking war-torn, highways and city streets resembled packed parking lots. Abandoned vehicles for one reason or another lined up in rows, some with doors open and windows blown out. Seeing all of this, I could only imagine how the fleeing experience could have been. Adults, some with children in tow, elderly people having to walk down long stretches of road, people of all ages and health trying to find shelter to save their own lives and others. Not all were successful.

So... When Do I See the Doctor?

For me to enter the city limits, I had to present proper iden-
tification to the authorities positioned at each entry point, as they
did not want anyone there who did not have to be. I was warned
that what I would return to might be unrecognizable to me. I
already considered that possibility before they mentioned it to me
at the checkpoint, but upon hearing their confirmation, I braced
myself even more.

As I approached my neighborhood, I saw ruin everywhere.
I looked around for landmarks to help me make sense of where I
was driving, something to remind me that once upon a short time
ago, those streets were busy with people living their lives. I noticed my neighborhood store in the distance but driving up to it
that day, I was not met with its usual massive presence. The
entire front was ripped off like Godzilla had reached down,
grabbed the face of the building, and flung it in the air without
caring where it landed.

I drove closer to my block, seeing entire lawns in front of
people's homes completely uprooted. Devastated is a word I
could use to describe my feelings driving down streets once so
familiar to me, but I am not sure if the word fully encapsulates the
myriad of shock waves running through me at that time. My heart
raced as I drove closer to my apartment building, and if I could
have covered my eyes for the big reveal, I would have. The "big
reveal" was almost unbelievable.

Astonishing that not even four blocks from that gutted
store, the trees on my block looked untouched. The lawn in front
of my building was green and alive, with no evidence of it trying to
hold on for life after being engulfed by drowning levee waters. I
was speechless. I had to look behind myself in the rearview mirror
to confirm that what I was seeing was real. When I averted my

eyes to the mirror, there it was behind me, unchanged: destruction and ruin. In front of me was as if my building and a couple of other blocks had not been through a thing. All exactly the way that I had left it a few weeks ago. I could not cry. I could not utter one word. I simply stared in awe of the Majesty that decided to put a saint-like umbrella over my home.

Parking in front of my building, I slowly got out of my car and looked around. Although there were a few neighbors who looked as if they were on the same mission — trying to process it all — I felt like the only person in the world. I accepted what I was seeing enough to enter my apartment building, but I still believed that it would be my apartment that was going to unveil the real damage. I knew this had to be the case, especially for me, because I lived on the ground level. The flooring of my building did not seem to have any traces of flooding, but I was still suspicious. Approaching my apartment door, I hesitated, preparing myself for the worst. I opened the door slowly, with only one eye open, and there was that familiar stillness that lingers after I have not been home in a while. Opening my eyes fully, I realized that the inside of my apartment had been just protected as the outside structure. Not one possession was out of place.

Of all the houses and businesses ripped from their foundations, cars flooded, flipped, and trampled, our beloved Charity Hospital never to be the same again, but my home was spared. So many lives lost, and I was permitted to live. So many doctors, nurses, and other staff in Charity Hospital and other facilities, fighting to save patients' lives with minimal resources. Had Charity declared their Code Gray emergency response at a different time, I, too, would have had to remain at or return to Charity Hospital. The staff who were placed on duty there and the patients they served would go on to experience some of the most agonizing ordeals any human being could have to endure. A week later, when some physicians and nurses in certain areas were being assigned cabins on ships to live in so they could continue to serve on the front lines for the hurricane's aftermath, Emory was devising a way for me to continue with them in Atlanta, for there was a different purpose for me there. At every turn, I was literally guided out and away from the storm.

I was kept away from possible death during Hurricane Katrina. Although I did not have to stand on top of my car or house as the water kept rising, hoping to get rescued before I was possibly submerged, I was close enough to see and feel the trauma it caused. I still have cutting memories of driving to Ericka's, heart palpitating, beating a thousand miles a minute. I think about the streets and areas I knew well that were gravely affected. I can still see myself eating at certain restaurants, visiting friends in their homes, or attending crawfish boils or a fish fry. I had so many amazing, unforgettable memories there. I did not have to experience the worst of the hurricane there to feel a profound sense of loss. Like anyone who lived through the viciousness of the storm in some way, many of us had to grieve the fact that where we once lived, we would not reside anymore. Where we once worked, played, "made" groceries...we would not return to the same life. And this new reality or transition was not introduced to us in a comforting way; rather, it was thrown at us the way my neighborhood store's facade looked like it was discarded: haphazardly and without care. We felt violated, like coming home to find everything in your house stolen or it burned down. My apartment might have still been intact, but due to the abrupt circumstances, I still had to quickly leave it for good. The levels of trauma could be considered relative, but we all felt it.

Sitting in my apartment, I was half alert, half in a daze about the sequelae of Hurricane Katrina that I was witnessing in real time. There were simultaneous feelings of gratitude and guilt applying pressure within, trying to force themselves to coexist in my chest. My heart pounded because of what could have been, then I felt immediately guilty because of the favor that was given to me. There was no great sense of relief that was not countered by the equally penetrating barrage of "Why me?"

When I finally got everything packed and was on the road to Atlanta, possibly never to reside in New Orleans again, my drive was pensive and intense to say the least. I realized that all of us who experienced it in some way had our share of personal damage due to Hurricane Katrina. The entire episode made it so people's experiences varied in intensity and manner, yet the storm created a community among us, if only by degrees of separation. For any who survived it, there was great reason for it, even if it was to be able to share the story with someone else. For me, I believe that I was spared because my professional and personal purposes had to do with what was ahead of me. I was fortunate to be taught and groomed by some of the best physicians in the country at one of our nation's most historic hospitals until the time when a storm nearly wiped it away. I do not take my lessons lightly, and I chose to enter my new phase in Atlanta excited and determined to give it all that I had.

So... When Do I See the Doctor?

T wo days prior to traveling to Atlanta, I had a talk with my dear friend Candace who I had befriended years ago in Indianapolis. Although she was not in Georgia, when she heard that I was going to arrive earlier than expected, she wanted to usher in a welcome wagon for me. Because of what I had just experienced, I was game for it.

Candace's "offering" was for me to become acquainted with someone new. "He's a really great guy who can show you Atlanta," expressed Candace with a smile over the phone. His name was John, and Candace and he were well acquainted because John had played on the same NFL team as Candace's future husband had; the two men had remained great friends.

It did not take long for me to warm to John after Candace, he, and I joined in on a call. John was smart, funny, and cool. We met in person the day I arrived in Atlanta, and just like that, we began hanging out. He was God-fearing, easy to talk to, and was driven and goal-oriented like I was. It also didn't hurt that he was easy-on-the-eyes. I must admit, my Cupid Candace made a good match.

While my personal life in Atlanta had gotten off to a solid start, my professional one was not flowing as much as past "first years" had. At Emory, there was confusion with my clinical rotations because I was mistakenly scheduled for two separate rotations at the same time. I was considered a "no-show" for the Rheumatology Clinic because I was present elsewhere. The attending rheumatologist charged at me over the phone, upset because I had not provided her coverage. I would never intentionally ignore or abandon any responsibility I was given, and my track record exemplified only that. Despite my attempts to reason with her, she would not let it go. By nature, I am a "keep my cool" kind of personality, but after she continued to rant for what seemed like forever, I finally riposted, "I heard you the first five times. You're beating a dead horse." Then, I hung up on her. As soon as I did this, I knew I was in trouble.

The next morning, I received a call from the Dean's office requesting a meeting with him the following day. As soon as the meeting was set, I spent the entire day creating a new career plan for my life because I was sure that I was going to be kicked out of the residency program. There is a lot to be said about a young Black female resident considered to be undermining and irresponsible.

I had never been in trouble in elementary school, middle school, high school, college, master's program, medical school, NEVER. I have never been considered disrespectful and didn't "talk back" to authority figures. Had never been summoned to the principal's office, let alone been labeled as a "troublemaker." The whole idea of having to see a superior due to something that I had done wrong was a novel experience for me. By the time I walked into the Dean's office after being told by his secretary, "He will see you now," I had already chosen my next career.

The moment I walked in, the Dean, an older White male, offered me a seat in front of his desk, where he sat. I looked around the room as I lowered myself onto the leather, academic chair. Shelves of books and a wall of accolades surrounded us to prove to anyone that whatever he deems, it will be the law. I was a bit nervous at first, as there were no pleasantries exchanged between the two of us. The only thing between us was his large wooden desk, most likely hand-carved many years before he was even born. He was very matter of fact and got straight to the point:

"Kimberly, I received a call from one of your attending physicians saying that she called you when she realized that you hadn't shown up to her clinic a couple of days ago. She said that when she told you how upset she was, you explained that you were in another clinic that day based on the schedule that was given to you. She then told you how extremely busy rheumatology clinics are and how they need every resident that they can get, and that your absence made it even tougher for them. She said at that point, you replied to her, 'I heard you the first five times. You're beating a dead horse.' Kimberly, did you in fact say that to your attending physician?"

Without hesitation, I looked him directly in his eyes and respectfully responded, "Yes, Sir, I did," all the while thinking about how I was going to explain to my mother that the one thing she warned me about when I was a teenager would be the thing to get me kicked out of residency — my "sometimes-too-honest," straightforward opinion. Mom's forecast was usually much less formal. Her words were:

"Your mouth is going to get you in trouble."

Though my mother's warnings were referring to our mother-daughter relationship, it would be new that I was so straight forward with someone else. Upon hearing me not at all deny what happened, the Dean stood up and walked around to the side of the desk where I sat, then he positioned himself on the edge of it to face me more directly. "Here it comes," I told myself. Like a lightning strike, the Dean jolted me with an uninhibited laugh so loud, as if I just told him one of the funniest jokes he ever heard.

"Kimberly, listen to me. You had a valid point, but either there is a better way of making your point or sometimes not trying to make your point at all. Starting tomorrow, go to the clinic that you have been in, and I will place someone else in the Rheumatology Clinic. And, Kimberly, I don't ever want to see you back in here again."

His words were as simple as that, and he never did see me in his office again. That experience was the start of my understanding the art of how and when to express my opinion. I humbly admit that my time with the Dean was my first lesson with learning how to curb my comments, but there would be a second.

I was a proud doctor at Emory. And I believe to this day about anyone: To know how someone truly feels about what they do, simply watch how they do it, and that will say it all. This was certainly true for me. I was always on time or early, I listened to wisdom, and I took copious notes. I believed that every step I took would get me closer to becoming that purposeful physician that God spared me in New Orleans to evolve into.

Since the encounter with the rheumatologist, I had kept a squeaky-clean record. It was not until a second infraction happened that I allowed myself to be tripped up again. This incident made me realize it wasn't so much my mouth needing to be controlled, as it was my need to learn how to not be triggered.

Later that same year during my oncology rotation, one of the nurses, an older White female, repeatedly griped within my earshot that she was tired of having to follow the orders of "new doctors who think they know everything." She added that she hadn't served as a nurse for decades only to have to take the orders of someone who "just started learning what to do." A few days later, during rounds in the presence of my attending physician and another resident, that same nurse made another snide comment. I was triggered. Right back at her, I fired, "I never told you that you couldn't be a doctor!"

Like the rheumatologist who was shocked at my clap back at her, this oncology nurse was instantly silent and stunned. The attending oncologist shot a look at me above the rim of his glasses then quickly returned to reviewing the abnormal labs I had presented to him moments before the nurse's comments. From that, my mind escaped to wonder if any pharmaceutical companies were hiring new representatives.

We all continued our rounds together, much of it quieted while my fellow resident stole glances of me in wonderment, and the nurse did the same, only hers were full of venom.

I did not get reprimanded by anyone for my rebuttal of the nurse; instead, I alone reprimanded myself. Not having been approached by anyone made me feel worse, and not because I felt my perspective was wrong. I absolutely had the right to feel a certain way about someone trying to define who I was as a doctor and what that position meant to me. Who was she to speak to me like that? I did not attend over ten years of school after high school just to have an inflated ego and tell people what to do, nor did I think I knew everything. I was a notetaking, open-eared resident who listened intently to our attending physicians, fellow residents, and any other member of the medical team. I took pride in learning. From what I had witnessed and experienced thus far, physicians and nurses can have an incredible rapport and relationship, with both appreciating and respecting one another and understanding how different and valuable each one's skillsets benefit patients. That nurse was contentious and sought to create tension. Deep down she was unhappy with what she brought to the table and tried to impose that wicked demeanor on me, thinking I would take it in because I wasn't yet "established" there. Because I was "new." I let her win by triggering me, which is why I felt worse. Never again would I allow someone else's low vibrations to affect my own high ones. I strive every day to ascend in my profession. It is an inalienable right of all people, regardless of what they do or how long they have been doing it.

As I mastered the ability to keep myself in check for the haters that would come and go, the ongoing strength I had to muster to get through my years as a resident due to my mother's recent cancer diagnosis was a journey of twisting and turning I never thought I would have to endure. Until that point, my father's passing was the worst trauma that I'd ever felt, making my heart feel like it had been ripped out of my chest. With my mother, it felt like after God put my heart back in its place again, her situation did not completely shock it all at once, rather it repeatedly and relentlessly tased it. Each call about my mother's deteriorating health took more out of me.

Unlike prior to my Daddy's transition, with Mom, I had time to reflect on our relationship and consciously appreciate it, knowing her days were limited. I was able to cry some nights, realizing that the day would come when God would call her Home. I am so grateful to my Aunt Louise and my sister Ericka for being at Mom's side until the end. God knows who to call forth and when.

My mother's condition had a profound emotional toll on me during residency, though I was still able to remain professional while waiting on the sidelines as the most important person I loved on earth declined. My "Number One Superhero" was becoming mortal.

My mother died of brain cancer on November 17, 2008, before I completed my residency program. I know she was and continues to be with me. When I need a good pep talk or word of encouragement, I imagine the soothing voices and wisdom from both she and my dad to help me finish strong.

Like my father's, my mother's funeral was also a joyful celebration of who she was. Everyone from siblings, extended family, friends, and colleagues flooded the church. Seeing all of this ignited a light within Ericka and me. It was so endearing to see everyone saluting my mother's life and contributions to the world. I was able to hold it together until my mother's Delta sorority sisters sang the final song during her Omega Omega service. The closing of her casket punctuated the reality that she was really gone.

Returning to Atlanta from Louisiana, I was prepared to feel the same void I did after Daddy passed. Grief never disappoints. It was so difficult for me to get out of bed, let alone do rounds with the team. And as my life would have it, not long after Mom's funeral, I was scheduled to take the United States Medical Licensing Examination (USMLE) Step 3, a key exam to moving onward as a physician. For this exam, you are only allowed a limited number of attempts to pass.

I was not ready in any sense of being prepared. I was having an incredibly tough time emotionally, which made it difficult to focus enough to study for anything. This time in my life felt almost impossible to overcome, but I still had to take the exam. So, with an absent state of mind, I blindly took my first shot and failed.

After finding out my inevitable score, I began to, yet again, strategize my potential new career. John coached me up, reminding me that I could and would pass the exam the second time. At the same time, he comforted me by telling me that, pass or fail, he had my back.

For my mother's passing, I chose to accept one month of the bereavement time offered by the program. During that time, I studied twelve hours a day at my neighborhood bookstore, taking a food break in between. I put a battery in my back, and I was on a mission.

I passed my second attempt at the USMLE Step 3 exam. There was a sigh of relief that only my mother and father could have understood because I know they reached from Heaven to give me all they had to ensure I would take our family legacy to the next level. Exit Resident Doctor Gilbert, enter Physiatrist Dr. Kimberly Gilbert.

7

The Practice

"Out of adversity comes opportunity."
- Benjamin Franklin

Hindsight is indeed 20/20, especially when thinking about the lessons you are given throughout your life. This old cliché has proven so true for me. Looking back, I understand why after years of being uplifted by family and friends as a child, I had to encounter my first real detractor in my teens. It was a test to determine how strong I had been built to persevere despite being ambushed by a shocking bomb of criticism about a career choice I had not, until moments before I was told, "You are not smart enough to be a doctor," had the willingness to share. In the end, I was not broken, and I created my own path and earned the right to add "MD" to my name.

Mr. George may never know the unintended role he played in my success.

Now, as an adult, the two left field run-ins I would later have during residency with fellow medical professionals, one challenging me about my diligence and the other imposing her own personal issues upon me, were also preparing me for the world I would enter post-residency.

Until that time, most of the adversity I experienced derived from my own creations. The interesting choice of college I selected as a pre-med student, the study method I chose the first time I prepared for the MCAT, even my detour to Indianapolis — all choices I had made. Therefore, any challenge that arose from these choices, no matter how difficult, did not stir undue stress in me. As a former athlete, I am used to challenges, but the challenges are in a big way, also expected. Athletes don't just run out onto a field or court without first knowing the playbook and the competition. We are trained, coached up, prepared for damn near any move made that might come our way to prevent us from winning. Sometimes there is an unexpected move, but I always knew how to call an audible. Strength, skill, intelligence, integrity, and endurance were key tools I used to overcome.

These same tools are key when navigating life in general, except there are so many ways for a challenge to present itself that we cannot possibly be prepared for all the ways that opposition can arise. And no level of "coaching up" can spare someone from being surprised by parts of it. As Mike Tyson declared years ago, "Everybody has a plan until they get punched in the mouth." The real objective here is being able to get back up after the wind is knocked out of you by a blow you did not see coming. I succeeded with Mr. George's attempt to tear me down, but there would be additional ones to follow for reasons more complicated than I wasn't a teacher's pet, or I was playing for an opposing team. No, these would be coming from those with whom I worked and had built a familiar, comfortable, and respectful rapport; from those who worked where I did and who also looked like me — who I initially would think my role in the field would make them feel proud; from those who perhaps assumed I was not as smart as my earned profession should explain; even audaciously from those who needed my professional expertise. During these moments, when important factors like race and gender different from the status quo are highlighted, all the gloves come off.

My climb up the medical mountain was built on being mostly prepared for adversity. In the real life of being a doctor, though, adversity can suddenly appear without warning. But guess what? I had been through so much already, there was nothing unforeseen that I was afraid to confront.

My residency could not have ended at a better time for me to have to prove that I had indeed learned from my many lessons, than to happen in the middle of a recession. The year 2009 was an extremely difficult time for virtually every industry. The finance world was crushed, which affected everything and everyone. People lost their jobs, their homes, their entire livelihoods. While others were trying to hold onto their lifestyles and assets they had already acquired, I was ready to build my own. I had yet to establish much due to years of laser focused dedication in preparation to be a physiatrist. Still, I had to keep in mind the financial climate around me and approach my search for a new job with a vigilant, purposed, and prudent mind.

Even the medical world was hit with the shade of the recession, so competition was even higher in this new skeletal market because there was not the typical list of opportunities waiting for me. I eventually found a few promising opportunities, and the one that showed the most was a private practice located just an hour outside of metro Atlanta. "The Practice" seemed to offer almost everything I was interested in. The physicians and high-level administrators with whom I spoke exuded great enthusiasm for bringing me on the team. The base salary they were offering to pay was typical for what a physiatrist post-residency would earn, so I was happy that I was not being low-balled. The morning after my interview, an offer of employment was emailed to me. I was eager to sign and get started.

During a weekend brunch a few days after receiving my offer, I shared the good news with one of my most trusted attending physicians from Emory, but she did not seem pleased. We talked about how to best secure a job during the recession, and she advised me to counter The Practice's offer with a $100k increase. I nearly spit out my water. "You do realize we are in a recession, Doc. Many physicians are having major challenges even getting a job, much less not having to accept these mid-recession, Lilliputian salaries!"

Doc was a fellow Louisiana native, and our shared roots gave us a common ground and ease of communication from the day we met. She was an excellent physician, and I looked up to her immensely. Doc's words were resolute.

"Trust me, Kim. They know your worth. They will accept it."

To ensure that I followed her fearless strategy, which returned me to my pre-recession standard level of courage, Doc stood over me and watched me type out my counteroffer all the way up until I pressed "Send." I always appreciated Doc for giving me such sound advice. This act of positive reinforcement proved even more helpful because the recession had inspired fear and uncertainty in many people, including me. What was happening around us was a very real thing, but there were those who refused to give in and pushed the envelope anyway. Doc had no hesitation to do this, and she knew I had it in me, too. I know she would not suggest for someone to so boldly counter at that time if she did not think they were built for it. I followed her lead with all the optimism and hope that I could as I typed:

"Hello,

Thank you for your offer. I would like to join the team but given the dedication and expertise I know I will provide, I cannot accept anything less than (the new amount)."

I held my breath and clicked *"Send."*

To my surprise, the CEO replied within fifteen minutes. I fixated on his first word for a while before I finished reading the rest:

"Done. Here is the revised offer with your requested salary. We are very excited to have you as a part of our team."

He had begun his response with "Done." Whoa. It worked. When Doc read his reply, she nodded with approval, sipped her tea, then said:

"Kim, there are two things I want you to always remember: First, know your worth. And second, a closed mouth does not get fed."

When she told me this, in my mind I said, "Done."

Interesting that right when I accepted the offer from The Practice, I also received an offer from a well-respected group of physiatrists in Metro Atlanta who wanted to bring me on as a "fellow for a new program" in their private practice, which was another way of saying that I would be expected to do more work for less pay. Soon after, I learned that another resident physician in my program who I told about this job opportunity had whispered in the ear of another physiatrist to apply for the same position. When I learned she had done this to me, I felt more than betrayed. For the countless times during the three years we worked together as residents when I stood in the gap for her after she would plead with me to cover for her because she would not be able to make it to work on time or when she wanted to skip out for a while and then return later in the evening while we were on call, put a bad taste in my mouth. "Can you please cover for me?" she would ask. Time after time, I did, and never spoke a word to anyone. What she did to me now was disdainful. More important than her backstabbing, I was not the type to broadcast information to people without having myself covered in some way — I never put anything past anyone. While she thought I was completely vulnerable to what I had told her, I had already secured a job with The Practice and respectfully declined the opportunity in Metro Atlanta. She was attempting to use that inside information from me to make her look good to fellow physicians with whom she wanted to be aligned. Her duplicitous act was dishonorable. She was willing to use me by sharing a job opportunity she believed I needed to continue my career, in order to boost her own. The physician she tipped off had more honor than her, though. Finding out through someone else that I had initially interviewed for the job, he called me to be sure that I had passed on the opportunity before he applied for it. I thanked him for the integrity he showed towards me, was proud to tell him that I had already secured a job, then blessed his efforts to land that position.

What I learned about that experience is that going forward, I would encounter two types of people in my career: Those who were on my team and those who were not, even if they initially pretend to be.

My new job at The Practice was an hour drive away, yet I did not mind because I had the company of my favorite morning radio shows that acted as my voices of entertainment and upliftment to help start my day each morning. I enjoyed the drive on the way to work as well as the ride back home listening to my favorite songs, my time to unwind. And, fortunately, I was usually driving opposite the busy Atlanta traffic.

As the first Black physician, as well as the first female physician hire, every day I reported to a team of thirteen White male surgeons, all of whom were welcoming and warm from the start. I believed they considered it a good thing that a woman who could also be "one of the boys" had joined the team. One by one, many of them took on roles of "Big Brother" to varying degrees, and I embraced this, because it is in my nature as a physician and in general to be excited about how I can grow and learn something new. I had warmed to some of the administrative staff as well, and as time went on, I thanked my lucky stars for being in this position during the tough economic times. As the days went on and everyone became very familiar with me, I was invited to start attending The Practice's quarterly financial meetings, growing increasingly impressed with what I saw on paper which confirmed what I was bringing to the table and how my skillset was benefitting the practice. The team thought so, too, and for my hard work (so I believed) my likeness was integrated within their marketing strategy. They put me, their new "lottery pick," front and center.

Early on, my Emory attending physician, Doc, advised me to challenge the initial offer given to me by $100k. This advice was suggested at the height of the recession, a major financial crisis in America. She told me to "know my worth." I took heed and received what I asked for — during a financial collapse. Doc's positive reinforcement brought me back to the Kimberly Gilbert I always was — unafraid to push the envelope — and when, after a period of time I realized during those financial meetings just how much my contributions were earning The Practice, I decided to speak up again. A closed mouth does not get fed.

When it was time to renegotiate my contract, I not only asked for an increase of my base salary but also an increase in the percentage of what I knew my specific work was profiting the business. The response to my requests were, at best, a pat on the head. I was asked by Jim, the CEO, to "go ahead and just renew" my rookie contract without any changes because they could "always amend it at any time as soon as it was approved." I countered to Jim, asking if they felt that I was in fact not worth the changes. He offered me another pat on the head, saying, "Oh, you're definitely worth it! You're great. We're just waiting for Dr. Garrett to come back in town from vacation because he's a partner who also has to approve any changes."

I waited patiently for the two weeks to pass before the remaining "approving" Dr. Garrett returned from vacation, and then gave them another week to "discuss" it. Poised to continue with our previous conversation about my contract, as soon as I reminded Jim about our agreement to revisit my contract amendments when Dr. Garrett returned, Jim turned on me. He told me that the partners had an issue with my disposition with the staff. In over two years, this, among other new criticisms he suddenly shared, was my first-time hearing from the physician team about anyone's displeasure with me or anything I did there. I was stunned, and a bit hurt. Not until I asked for more compensation that I knew I deserved — based upon exponentially inclining figures that were a result of the hard work that I was doing there — had I ever been met with any condemnation or feelings about staff expressing dissatisfaction about me or how I performed as a physician. No one on the "team" ever so much as commented on a hair I had out of place — because there weren't any. The non-physician staff, largely comprised of White women, often took petty shots at me. But I deflected those with gentle laughs, as I always chose to take the high road. And because of how I handled these encounters, they were never mentioned to me by the fellow physicians. I stayed on my toes to not be caught vulnerable, as this wasn't my first time dealing with certain types of people.

Before starting this new job, I knew that I had to, in various ways, prepare for the environment. When working in a predominately White space, Black people know in advance all the rules we must follow. Medical school was the start of me revisiting those age-old lessons shared with Ericka and me: You have to get up earlier in the morning, work at least twice as hard, and then, only then, might you be considered "somewhat equal." I knew I was now in a world where my outshining achievements could be downplayed if those achievements outshined a White person's own, or if those achievements justified asking them for more money. Work hard, but quietly. Be clear and serious but be aware that being perceived as "too serious" will in their eyes earn you the "Angry Black Woman" label. I knew to be careful and always had been. Be proud but gracious. I was always cordial and professional and had never had any infractions there despite the shots taken at me by the non-physician staff. I was all these things, but I was also not a fool and was not going to allow anyone to turn anything around on me to lock me out of something I absolutely deserved. Because I knew I had done nothing wrong, and my spirit was telling me that this criticism was rooted in a belief system that was created generations before me, rather than submit, I chose to defend myself then cut my losses so that I could move on.

"Oh okay, so we don't need to renew my contract. You all can look for a physiatrist that your staff feels fits in."

Jim looked shocked that I would "say such a thing." For all I had already been through, I was not surprised I had responded so resolutely. I was quite calm and confident, like Dr. Rebecca Crumpler, when she was mistreated at the Freedmen's Bureau and chose to valiantly reinvent herself and independently forge her own new path. To Jim, I might have come across as cavalier, but truthfully, I was simply holding onto my integrity. I did not exactly know my next professional move when I spoke up for myself, but I knew that I was not about to be pinned in a corner. Given a chance to redo that moment, I would say it again, because I meant it. I was willing to let it all go and start afresh someplace else. I had worked too hard.

I had no tangible proof that the exchange I was then having with Jim was rooted in what my spirit was telling me it really was. That's the funny thing about racism. People can be racist towards you with action, knowing that unless there is "solid proof," all they have to do is deny it and they will be absolved. Both of you might know what the truth is, but the offender never has to own up to it. This allows them the liberty to act this way toward

many others, unless and until a trend builds with the same blatantly discriminatory treatment toward the same type of people,
and then there might be a chance of justice being served. If a job
or salary is on the line, this can be even more of a challenge. Up
until that point, I was moving with a deep, uncomfortable feeling
inside that began elevating to the surface the more Jim spoke.
While I cannot pinpoint a previous time when something like this
had happened to me, there were a lot of similar moments that
resembled it — as we say today, microaggressions. I was not
reared to be afraid of anyone, regardless of race. But I was taught
to understand that there are those who would think they were
better than me because of our different races or genders, and
they would do anything they could to ensure that I did not ascend
because of it. Sometimes, it would manifest as them being okay
with me having a certain position or earning a certain amount of
money, as long as it was not near, at, or more than theirs. Elders
have encouraged me to be aware when it happens but, better yet,
do my best not to let it.

This move by The Practice was straight out of the racism
and sexism playbook. To use something as vague as my "disposition" against me was classic. Still, I had no proof to label his
behavior. I was also not brought up to pull the "race card;" most
Black people are not. I had to be cool, because all that had happened up until then between the other physicians and me was
that I was highly respected and liked — until I asked for more
money. I would never ignore or deny an opportunity to be better
where it applies. Before this moment, there were zero problems
with anything I did, said, or how I was performing professionally —
until I asked for a higher compensation that The Practice's own
financial records clearly illustrated that I deserved. As a matter of

fact, other practices in the area would refer their own spine and neurological patients to me due to my expertise. I was so highly favored that my "melanated" face was chosen to grace the pages of their marketing materials. How did I overnight become persona non grata? And if I had been erring in the ways that I was being told for the first time at that moment, why not tell me at each point when they happened? Why not pull me to the side, "Big Brother?" Why not whisper the critiques as they came so I could maintain balance for the team? Why keep constructive criticisms away from any staff that could potentially damage the morale of the office or the reputation of the business until an opportunity to use it as a weapon when the request of heightened compensation arises? For any owner who wants his or her business to thrive, I find that to be a questionable tactic. I am sure that in hindsight, Jim wished he could have found a way to keep me out of those financial briefings because it would have likely taken me longer to find out the information. The details I read clearly endorsed my value to The Practice. I walked in the door of that establishment as a new employee with a higher salary than they were initially offering me. Why would they think I would be satisfied with that forever, especially since I had been reading with my own eyes that, by each patient I saw, my financial value to them was growing so greatly? I had lots of questions and a gut feeling, but no "proof" that this was, in fact, racism and a textbook chauvinistic play.

"NO, we still want you here!" Jim said. "We just want you to keep the same contract."

And there was my proof. If I remained a quiet, "grateful" employee, they were willing to let me keep my job, newly mentionable flaws, and all — if I kept my contract the same. Yet, if I did not comply, they had a list of judgements and complaints —

criticisms that they would readily share. The hypocrisy was palpable. If that response from Jim did not confirm my innermost thoughts…

If my ethics, integrity, disposition, or skills were legitimately of concern, I do not think they would want me representing their practice at any salary. Jim, the CEO, was making it plain this was not about anything that had any merit at all. This was about control, and about keeping a Black woman "in her place." I looked around me at the other physicians there who were climbing up the practice ladder. They were all White. And all men. Yes, they did have other medical staff, but they were mostly comprised of White women. And the few Black people, who were happy to have their jobs, never made waves. In my heart, I knew what Jim was asking me to do. I knew this also meant that I would have to "play high school" with many of the immature staff members if I wanted to get them on my side. I damn sure wasn't going to play that game.

Fortunately, the incident happened on a Wednesday, which was one of John and my date nights. From the moment he saw my face, he could tell there was something wrong. He already had a clue because he had listened to me throughout the weeks talking about my impending contract renewal and my concerns for it to be amended, as well as what had been going on the two plus years I was there. "I'm working my ass off there, and they know it, but they don't want to honor it." John listened to me intently, then looked me in my eyes and got straight to the point.

"What do you want to do?"

John spoke with a measured tone, but there was an underlying tone of frustration. For anyone who is being mistreated, it is an anguishing feeling for loved ones to witness. John deserved to feel frustrated and angry for me, because how The Practice treated me was not fair. We knew in our hearts and minds that the sole reason for my mistreatment was due to race and gender bias. Again, the physician team was all White men on purpose, and their choice to "diversify" their practice by bringing me on board checked not one, but two, quota boxes. When companies opt to, either by pressure or to not become pressured, bring in the one or two "token" employees to look "diverse" or "equal opportunity," they do not expect for that employee to complain. Said employee should remain faithful and appreciative, and when they are not perceived as such, they can be threatened with demotion or termination. It was obvious that I was one of those "token hires," but I was unwilling to allow my bosses to pin me down with intimidation. In another era, I might be called an "Uppity Negro." John understood my plight because, as an entrepreneur and former professional athlete, he had experienced his own marginalization. In him, I had a solid ally who never asked me to compromise who I was. John also knew my worth and, yet again, had my back. I was proud that our relationship was not tied to any business move either of us made, especially if it challenged our core beliefs. I knew I had hit a ceiling at The Practice and wanted out. It felt good to have a partner who believed in me enough to ride my wave.

At The Practice, the waves that tried to sweep me off my island of self-respect culminated with my contract debacle, but it did not begin there. In hindsight, I only wish there would have been at least one on-the-side conversation with someone while I was still a medical student or resident physician about what I was destined to experience. What should be discussed with all female students and residents as well as students and residents of color on their way into the complicated world of medicine, is the level of marginalization you will receive from both colleagues and patients, and how to effectively navigate those waters. In many people's eyes, I am a double "negative," being both Black and female. And I had to, as many others who look like me in some way, handle each situation on my own, hoping that my tone or choice of words to simply protect myself were not at the same time "offending" anyone. My well-experienced, new doctor self was not fully prepared for those fellow physicians who would try to cleverly discriminate against me or the patients who refused to believe that I am the physician they are scheduled to see.

I will share with you my experience with my very first patient at The Practice, that was both eye-opening and utterly offensive. But for me to hold onto my new position, I had to roll with the punches.

Receiving a new patient is a process I knew all too well by that point in my career, and as usual, I entered the patient's room, greeted him with a smile and said, "Hello, I'm Dr. Gilbert...very nice to meet you." My patient, a White male, smiled back. I thoroughly reviewed his chart with him and discussed all his concerns. After our discussion, I proceeded to give my patient a comprehensive physical examination, reviewed his x-rays and other imaging studies with him, then shared my recommendations for improving both his medical condition and his overall quality of life. After this involved interaction, the patient commented, "That's a great plan." I was completely caught off guard by what he said next.

"Sooooo... when do I see the doctor?"

WHEN DO YOU SEE THE DOCTOR?

I had to chuckle to myself slightly to get past the sting, also trying to believe he was joking. I thought to myself, "He did hear me when I walked in an hour ago and introduced myself as Dr. Gilbert, the DOCTOR? My name matches what is on the schedule he read when he got his appointment letter in the mail, what he heard when the staff called and reminded him of his appointment, and what he was told again when he arrived today and checked in." If I had to recollect deeper about our exchanges during that detailed appointment, there is a possibility that he had not even looked me in my eyes until he asked me that audacious question. Achieving eye contact with me then was only for him to emphasize how much he meant what he said. Today, this ignorant display of marginalization still disappoints me to a degree, but unfortunately, I have had to develop very thick skin in order to prosper. "I am your doctor," I said with as much of a smile as someone slighted can accomplish, pointing to the "Dr. Kimberly Gilbert" perfectly embroidered on my long lab coat. His reply to my comment would proceed to test me more.

"Oh, you don't look like a doctor."

This prejudiced statement would be followed up with added ridiculousness from him as well as many other patients during different encounters throughout the years, like:

"You look too young."

"You're too pretty."

"You're too cool."

Imagine this level of unnecessary conversation as I was helping him — and countless others after him — improve their lives medically. If I were naive, there is a chance that I would have accepted these truly condescending statements as actual compliments. But because I had either worked with, or bore witness to, many younger-looking, attractive, and "cool" male physicians who were never mistaken for anyone other than a physician — even when they were not wearing their lab coat — I could not help but be offended.

What I did with that feeling is an unfair thing that anyone who is denigrated because of how they look must often do if they don't want to further complicate things and possibly risk losing their job: Don't complain. Suck it up. Get over it.

To become a physician, you spend innumerable hours and multiple years in preparation. For my journey from there to here, I not only lost one, but both of my parents, along the way. This has been by no means an easy feat. To finally arrive at the coveted space of earning my "MD," I did not consider the level of backlash, stereotyping, and countering I would receive.

Because there were a small number of genuinely good people sprinkled throughout the list of those who would insult me on a daily basis, I would use the respectful, kind ones as a little sunshine to brighten the constant discrimination storms I had to endure in order to maintain my strength and dedication. It was only because of those infrequent blasts of sunshine that I did not resign from The Practice earlier than I did.

It was the staff that would later serve as the prime reason why my professionalism came into question in the first place, the catalyst for compelling me to seriously consider leaving, which escalated my contract drama, and made me aware that I was not in a safe space.

From the moment I arrived at The Practice, there was a vying for my attention by the staff who "welcomed me in." And from the start, I felt uneasy with the energy that led it. Oh, the barrage of questions that ensued:

"Are you dating anyone?"

"I know you live in Atlanta, which is full of "open people," but you are dating a "he" right?"

"What does he do?

"What is his name? Oh, and his last name, too."

"Do you plan to get married?"

"What kind of wedding will you have and where will it be? You're going to move from Atlanta to here whenever you get married, right?"

"Do you want kids?"

"How many kids?"

"Boys or girls or both?"

"Will they go to private or public school?"

(Keep in mind, I was not even engaged when I started at The Practice).

"What are you doing after work?"

"Do you want to go have drinks with us?"

"Do you want to stay here this weekend and hang out with us?"

"Do you want to go to lunch with us?"

And on and on and on.......

I was the only Black physician, and the only female one, too. I don't think the staff knew what to do with me. And they certainly did not understand the art of tactfulness when questioning me, nor how to allow me the space to acclimate freely without having to feel poked and prodded. On many levels, I know why the caged bird sings.

So... When Do I See the Doctor?

Over time, I believe the staff could tell my level of discomfort, as I was never wordy with a response or accepted any of their invitations. I had gained a solid group of friends in Atlanta and never needed my work life to fulfill my social one. In my mind, I was there to be cordial and professional and do a stellar job as a physiatrist, which I walked in the door accomplishing. Yet, because I did not act like the "Grateful Negro," privileged to be included by them, they soon turned on me. The shade began with merely "group rebuffing" me when I arrived at the office, which was quickly followed up with interfering with my business.

Sitting in my area of the clinic, I would wonder what was taking my patients so long to be escorted to the patient rooms for their work up, and many other delays with paperwork and in-house imaging that caused intentional hold ups. After experiencing a series of the staff's undermining efforts, I realized that they were intentionally delaying my patients from seeing me, which would significantly prolong my day. It is a wonder, with all the sabotage, how I ended up performing so well and increasing the revenue for The Practice as much as I did. When I started to question the staff about the lack of flow with my patients, they would give me the most egregious answers. "Oh yeah. We didn't know you wanted them to be taken to the room" or "Oh, we didn't know they were ready to get their x-ray."

Their behavior was so blatantly disturbing and problematic. But if I complained, I knew, that as a Black woman, I would be labeled as angry and uncompromising. Add to that the fact that the few Black women who were on the staff largely did not have my back. In their eyes, because I was making substantially more money than they were, which I had earned, I needed to be happy "with what I did have." Like every other physician in that practice, I deserved every single dollar earned through hard work. Yet, even in the eyes of those who looked like me but happened to be ranked lower professionally, I should not get "out of line." They were not proud that I had ascended to the levels that I had toiled so hard for. It did not matter how much schooling or residency training, I should still feel "blessed" like I was being given a handout by my White bosses, as if I was some sort of faithful slave. What certain slaves did not realize back then was that, they, too, had earned not only the scraps they were given to eat and survive but much, much more, although overseers would continuously instill in them that the overseer and Master were to be shown gratitude for them being "allowed" to exist. I was not a faithful slave, and I knew my worth.

I had stuffed the staff's insubordination in the back pocket of my scrubs for as long as I could, and I had put two and two together about my financial due. The help from the two Black women who in a quiet way had my back, the here-and-there respectful patients, the handful of White women in the building who would not bash me but when given the opportunity would not actually defend me, was not enough for me to remain at The Practice.

When the physician team tried to use all of this against me and I ultimately turned the contract back on them, this resulted in an even better financial outcome for me. If we are open, God always has a plan. I learned invaluable lessons at my very first job post-residency, and they earned a heck of a lot of money as a result of hiring me. For a time, everyone was seemingly winning. The moment I realized I had not really been winning at all, is when I had to walk away. And, I have zero regrets.

M y final hour-long commute back home, I listened to my usual soundtrack mixed with old school and new school, feeling good about my choice to move on. So many people who look like me end up stuck, trapped in work places and spaces that do not define them, spending hours a day placating to people who they know do not have their back, who would turn on them for a bonus or extra shift, brown-nosing higher-ups who don't respect their "kind" simply because these people hold the keys to helping them pay their bills or maintain a certain lifestyle. There are people who look like me who have families to take care of, student loans and other serious debt to satisfy. For many, it feels impossible to stand up for themselves because money is in the way. Money.

While I would still be at my previous place of employment if I had played the role of "grateful," what I am most grateful for is my ability to have a choice. Because of my own personal journey, I knew I did not have to take what I was being given. I had mentors, allies, and loved ones that, if I ever seemed like I was bending to intimidation, reminded me at every turn that I was worth more and had earned the right to demand more. Even with my level of credentials and better, there are still those Black people who continue to choose to take the shorter end of the stick. They do not want their livelihoods threatened. But if they are unceremoniously let go after years of "loyalty," what then could be said? I chose to and will always choose to bank on and believe in me. I know for sure that God has my back, and no one can get in the way of what is due to me if I do my part and hold onto my sense of courage to go for it.

Though I drove one hour back to my home in midtown

Atlanta, I felt like I was leaving decades behind.

8

The Agency

"The ones with knowledge are feared. The ones without, controlled."
- Unknown

J oining the "I have now been marginalized" club is not a membership anyone wants to obtain. Being able to share and compare stories about how you have been unfairly treated and how your life is now forever changed because of it, simply because you have — almost overnight — grown new sensory antennae specially designed to detect oncoming discrimination before it can impose the same potentially lasting and damaging effects as your initial experience did. These antennae are supposed to protect you, give you advanced notice, so to speak. No longer are you able to live naively, meandering through your world believing that doing your best will pay off, even on the front end, and that those who created the rules of "equality" meant to include people who look like you. "Work hard, gain the appropriate knowledge and skills, and based on pure merit you will succeed with no societal-driven opposition along the way." If you have earned the right credentials, the world must respect you for it, no matter who you are or what you look like. After all, America is a merit-based achievement system, right? Isn't this what the "Big Dream" is supposed to be about? Truth is, if you check any box other than White male, you might be in for a serious uphill battle to receive the earned respect and financial compensation for what you have worked hard to achieve.

This fact is not fatalistic, and this is not a "rant." It is simply the truth. It would be irresponsible for me to experience something so oppressive and not speak on it, pretending it does not happen, wishing it were a dream. One by one, as if it is some sort of rite of passage, our realms are being broadened with an uneasiness we did not ask for, a new way of thinking and understanding that we would rather not have had to acclimate to. There are those able to live their entire lives without major incident. They can go by "the book," and the book rewards them for it. I am part of a different group of people who routinely go by the book, and this can actually work against us. Me being a woman can create a double challenge. What happened to me at The Practice did not intimidate me to stop pressing forward. On the contrary, like many of those who have come before me and many others even today, the experience gave me a stronger sense of purpose, a different sort of "gift of sight," like seeing a red car on the streets for the first time, now suddenly you notice them everywhere.

I knew I would continue to ascend, but I also knew that I had to truly be on guard, lest there would be those poised to cripple me. This is the all-important fine print no one tells those who could be affected by discrimination to read. In other words, "The devil's in the details."

While preparing to leave The Practice, I considered new opportunities for the next phase of my journey. Through a connection with my former residency coordinator, I decided to join a physiatry group, "The Agency," who proclaimed that they would find and manage new opportunities for me. The idea sounded attractive because there was a stronger possibility for me to be more autonomous with my work. The agreement was The Agency would locate medical facilities where I would be consulted on patients undergoing physical rehabilitation, be a source of knowledge and guidance, and handle my billing for those services, for an agreed percentage of my reimbursement. The fact that there was a familiar connection established some sort of initial trust, which sped up my processing of this new offer to sign on with the team.

One of the physiatrists, Dr. Steve Jones, had been a resident in the same PM&R residency program. The two heads, Peter Bisset, CEO, and Dr. Miguel Morales, COO, were straight forward enough. All seemed completely empathetic to my previous experience at The Practice, and there was a resounding energy of being aghast about how I was treated there. Like confident agents selling a dream, they insisted that The Practice's behavior and way of doing business was behind me and they would show and prove just how proud they all were to have me be part of their team. All the bells and whistles they told me about the company sounded great, and they were not hesitant to express that because, according to The Agency, serving as my management company would guarantee consistent financial growth. They were first to speak about compensation without me having to pose a question about it. By all that they were saying, I was at ease, initially feeling that The Agency operated in stark contrast to The Practice. This new team and leadership were a breath of fresh air compared to where I had just come from.

I might not be quick to attend after-work cocktail hour when I start a new job, but professionally, I am always excited to hit the ground running. I was eager and prepared to begin working with the new medical facility I was paired with by The Agency. On my way to the first meeting with the staff, I looked forward to all the new patients I would soon be helping to regain their most optimal health.

I did find it interesting that upon arrival I was not formally introduced to the staff as the new physiatrist on board. And within a few more moments, Peter began a "presentation" that detailed how much the medical facility would benefit from having a physiatrist at their facility. This was not an introduction for a secured position, it was no more than a marketing ploy. A solicitation. I was dumbfounded to say the least and humiliated to say the most. How could they set me up that way? With nowhere to run, I had to pretend that I was privy to what was going on and sit through that "presentation" while Peter was trying to sell me as if I was some sort of show pony. I felt utterly embarrassed.

Knowing that it can take time to secure a consultant position at a medical facility, even if Peter had actually piqued sincere interest from the CEO at that medical facility with his presentation (which, he did not), I would not be brought on overnight. I spent my first five weeks being "managed" by The Agency without a job, forcing me to use a portion of my hard-earned savings to pay bills. Who opts for that when you are supposed to be working, and you are not the reason for your lack of employment? Thank goodness for a clause I had strategically put in my rookie contract with The Practice, which fortunately had given me a nice financial cushion. I am grateful that I was raised to hope for the best and prepare for the worst. As for The Agency, I was incensed, but I did not leave. Fool me once, shame on you.

Absurdly, the second and third facilities I was linked with by The Agency had also not formally signed on to add a physiatrist to their medical staff before my introduction, but the silver lining in these cases was, the moment I realized The Agency was trying to play the "okey doke" on me again, I immediately relinquished my dependence on them to close the deal and morphed into 100% self-reliant mode.

Speaking with the CEOs on my own, both kind and intelligent middle-aged minority men, they listened to me intently as I shared with them some of the key benefits that my services could provide. The CEOs and I had pleasant and informative dialogues, with them sharing about their facilities as well. The result of their open-mindedness was that they did sign on to having me. I worked with these facilities for many years, and to this day, both open-minded CEOs and I continue to be friends.

Still a part of The Agency's roster, I had thus far been led to three medical facilities, and though I signed on with the second and third ones, the only credit anyone at The Agency could take was finding the locations and botching the first consulting "opportunity" that was never even real. So, when I was approached by them to contract at a major Atlanta hospital as their fourth attempt to land something for me, serving as Medical Director of the Acute Inpatient Rehabilitation Unit, I was leery. This job was actually secured, I assumed, because I was replacing someone who was stepping down, which suggested there was actually a position available.

The Agency might have finally secured an actual position for me, but it was one where I walked on land mines all day. I never knew where to step to prevent getting bombed. For starters, my predecessor, a White male who had served in this position for over 22 years, was extremely beloved, so much so that there was a portrait of him hanging on the wall so center stage that it seemed like no matter where I turned, I could not help but see it. His aura was not the problem. In fact, he was quite kind and helpful during our conversed transition of power, and he kept his door open if I ever had any questions. The nurses and therapists, however, were all young-to-middle-aged White women who also doubled as members of my predecessor's lifetime fan club, and they were menacing. In their eyes, there was nothing I could do right — my mere presence in the building was wrong. I was a constant reminder to them every day that I was not him.

As opposed to being protected as the head of the department, instead I felt like I was in a perilous space. Every day, I walked into that environment as if I were in a war zone, constantly having to defend myself as much as I was able to work. Too many of the usual tactics of sabotage to name: the typical insubordination, lack of teamwork when it came to caring for patients, and a battery of excessive undermining that would make your head spin. Less than six months there, I had enough.

I shared with Peter, Dr. Jones, and Dr. Morales my concerns and imperative need to leave, and together they all seemed to understand my plight. While I thought they were making preparations for my exit, I received a tip from an ally within the hospital that they were actually telling both the CEO and COO of the hospital that they were "smoothing things over" with me so that I could remain working there. I had spoken freely to them, sharing specific details about the double standards, hypocrisy, and downright racist treatment. These scenarios that I explained were so blatant, they could not be described or perceived as anything but discrimination. Yet, behind my back these three were being deceitful, sympathizing with those who had been causing me undue stress, assuring them that under the current conditions I would stay?

From my understanding, they were not even trying to create a better situation for me there. I called Dr. Jones, my friend and colleague who was also one of the partners in The Agency, and I gave him the opportunity to tell me the truth about how they represented me to the hospital.

As physicians, we take an oath to practice medicine with integrity, and me calling Dr. Jones directly was my attempt at reminding him that this mentality of having integrity should extend to the guidelines of his managerial advice, and more importantly, our friendship. I believed that with the previous years spent together in residency he would have come clean. I understood none of the partners wanted me to quit the hospital simply because of how much money I generated for The Agency from that location alone, and they were all due their agreed percentage. But after our conversation, I hoped he would understand how detrimental it would have been to my career and professional reputation if I remained working in that toxic environment. There would be no way he would allow such deceptive actions to be made against me. I believed that given our recent group conversation where I gave them my truth, he would tell me the truth of what had been going on. He did not.

With this clarity, I only agreed to stay on as medical director because the CEO of the hospital expressed to me an urgent need for me to remain on board until they were able to find a replacement. Despite the conspiracy that was happening around me, I chose to do what many people would not do to prevent the acute rehabilitation unit from potentially being shut down. I continued working through the fire for an additional three months. The year was 2014, and I have not spoken a word to my "friend" and old colleague, Dr. Jones, since.

Successive inexcusable actions from The Agency all culminated with me having to walk away, such as, they failed to follow through on their initial "agent sell" to me: For an agreed percentage of my earnings, they would make my work seamless. They would align me with medical facilities and then handle all my billing that followed. They would be a source of knowledge and wisdom on how to navigate certain types of facilities that I had not previously worked in. Because of all the drama I was experiencing, it took a few months to notice that while I had fulfilled my end of the deal by working vigorously, deposits into my bank account had become sluggish. It turns out that a soured personal relationship between the not well-credited or well-vetted billing company and The Agency, who hired them, dismantled the entire financial system. Everyone involved with The Agency in a financial way suffered, including me. As opposed to being honorable and making me aware, Peter continued to be dishonest at every turn. After a month of his lies, I had enough and gave The Agency my notice to end our contractual relationship.

Eventually, John and I got everything straightened out but not without the frustration of having to chase back pay as well as locate unpaid claims. Because I had more legitimate issues with The Agency than I would have liked to speak of, I knew I had to move on. Thankfully, my sensory antennae had matured by then, and it did not take me as long as it did with The Practice for me to figure out how much I deserved to be in an environment that valued me and the work I did, as much I valued doing the work. Regardless of how much money you are making in your career, if you feel that your integrity and value are being compromised, you reiterate to yourself the wisdom that you can never get time back again, so do not allow people to waste it. Still early in my career, I had prepared my life to have options, and this did not include accepting being marginalized. I was not in a room full of White men this time, but they were still all men. They could all feel at ease at The Agency because they respected each other and knew they would protect one another. As a woman, I was extended no such courtesy. Fool me twice, shame on me. I was 'outta' there.

Fortunately, I was able to circumvent the non-compete clause in my contract to be able to continue with the second and third medical facilities introduced to me by The Agency, though they had absolutely nothing to do with my success there. When the CEOs were approached by Peter using the same previous solicitation presentation, the empty marketing ploy had fallen on deaf ears. Fortunately, they did not end the encounter outright. They were open enough to engage with me directly, and our sincere exchanges led to them accepting me as the team physiatrist, with our relationships being founded on mutual respect.

I felt great for the first time in a while. I understood why this was: I had become 100% independent. I was confident in my own manner of introducing and presenting myself to medical facilities, as I had already achieved success with two and was doing very well there. When I realized I could be self-reliant and successful at the same time, there was no stopping me. I began adding a new medical facility to my roster faster and more efficiently than any "agency" could, and I did not have to share my earnings with anyone but Uncle Sam.

Life was good. John and I were happily married, and by then were ecstatic to learn I was pregnant with twin girls. This blessing was particularly special news because I miscarried our first child just six months before. With all the work that I had been doing, as well as the unnecessary pressures at work, the loss took an emotional toll on me. I could not put into words how incredibly grateful I felt to have a second chance at motherhood.

I had hit a great stride by the time my pregnancy matured to my second trimester and being pregnant with twins did not slow me down. In fact, knowing I was housing not one, but two little humans, put a fire under me I never knew was there. As a working mother-to-be, everyday all you can think of is your need to be prepared to give your unborn child or children the best life you can provide. For me, I am not talking about just diapers, bottles, clothes, and toys. While still pregnant, I seriously started planning for college, apprenticeships, and generational wealth. I worked extremely hard for them.

My train was going full speed, and this was noticed by Dr. Stuey, the medical director of one of my medical facilities, and he asked to have a meeting with me. Just as he knew about me, I also knew about him. And what I knew, I was not very fond of. I did not have anything against him, but I was suspicious about what he wanted to discuss. Still, I agreed to meet with him.

He sat at the desk, his diminutive body nearly swallowed by everything around him in the office, and I chose to keep silent until he spoke first, which he took great pleasure in doing.

"I've been watching you. You are doing some great work here and around the city."

"Thank you."

"You have been here for several years now, and I understand the staff has taken well to you. And I hear your bedside manner with patients is excellent."

"Yes, thank you again."

He leaned back in the chair and gave me a patronizing once over. I envisioned him leaning back in his chair so much that he flipped over.

"With you working at so many other medical facilities, I am sure you must be feeling overwhelmed and overly extended at times. So why not join in with me? I run dozens of facilities all over Georgia. You could become my physiatrist, and for you, I'd pay top dollar."

The last time I checked, I had not considered myself a slave or a mare. "Top dollar," I thought to myself. "Who does he think I am?" Right away, in my head, I answered my own question: Despite how small, he is a man. And, in his eyes, I am "just a woman." And that explained everything. I entertained him a few minutes longer, responding "I am usually not so upfront about money, but how much are you talking about?"

Holding a pen between his two index fingers and thumbs, a move I imagined he had practiced his entire life, watching "executive villain films," he smugly answered me,

"Honey, what do you want to make?"

What a schmuck. He had no idea who he was talking to. I had just completed two long rounds of sexist drama by men of many shades. Him being Black, I felt no sense of devastation as he was, in real time, completing my discrimination spectrum.

There was no way I was working for him, not for keys to the U.S. Mint.

I paused for a few beats to make him believe that I was paying attention.

"Wow, that is quite an offer. Can I get back with you?"

"Of course, you can. You probably need to discuss this with the man of the house, which I totally understand. But don't wait too long!"

Schmuck was too kind a word for him.

His creepy smile rivaled any of the Jokers in the DC comics. I could not get out of there fast enough. My babies were listening to this clown!

About two days later, I sent him an email to give him the impression that I considered his lame offer:

"Good morning, Dr. Stuey. Thank you again for your offer. At this time, I think it is best for me to remain independent. If there is ever an opportunity for us to work together in the future, I look forward to it. Regards."

Relieved that I had just dodged a bullet, believing the encounter served as a test of my will to see if I would give in to yet another man who "decided" he should lead my career, only to disappoint me in the end. I woke up the next morning and headed to work, business as usual. While driving from one facility to the next, I received a call from Dr. Stuey's location being introduced to the new CEO of that facility. This new CEO spoke kindly, yet with caution, beginning with an apology for having to introduce himself in "this way."

"Excuse me?" I was puzzled.

"Well, I don't even know why he had me be the one to call you, but Dr. Stuey told me to inform you that he has decided to hire his own physiatrist. I'm so sorry."

"What in the world? Was I hearing correctly? I declined his offer just yesterday," I thought.

I knew this new CEO was only trying to do his job, and he did not deserve any negative tone from me, and I was not going to give him any.

"Alright...Can you tell me when I should begin my process to transition out?"

I heard a sigh on the other end of the phone, as if he were trying to muster the courage to speak.

"I am sorry again, Dr. Gilbert. Dr. Stuey said that this is effective immediately."

I thanked the new CEO, wished him luck, and hung up. I put my hand over my belly, feeling my daughters kicking as I thought about my next move. I whispered to them a promise that their livelihoods would never be dependent on such selfish, random actions of other people that could threaten their destiny.

So, this is what happens if you reject a misogynistic offer? As a woman, was my only option to let that man lead me or not have a job? His bruised ego was more important than me being able to provide for the babies he knew I was carrying. He was willing to take food out of their mouths to soothe his own inner issues. Up until that point, I expected the Asshole mentality, but Dr. Stuey had taken the term to a new low.

Just like that, I had joined the legions of women who had to experience the wrath of a fragile male ego that feels rejected. I was linking arms with women who are called "Bitch" because they refuse a man's advances, all of those women who are sexually harassed, or because they refuse to be sexually manhandled, watch their careers be ruined by angered, controlling, monstrous male counterparts. I was embracing the women who are unceremoniously fired because a man has decided they were too old or not appealing anymore, or those like me, whose independence, grit, resilience, and confidence are obviously too intimidating.

As I have mentioned throughout this story, I am too often considered a "double negative" — Black and female — but I do not consider these characteristics as something that makes me weaker. They have absolutely fortified me in more ways than even I will never know. I am reminded by the undisputed influences of women like Forever First Lady Michelle Obama, Oprah Winfrey, Rosalind Brewer, and Serena Williams, whose images remind me of who I am, and whose I am. I am also not misled by these highlighted names in our culture into thinking that Black females have "made it." These women serve as beacons to encourage us to persevere despite adversity, but their successes have not spared Black women in general from being marginalized and discriminated against. I am proof that your average achievement-driven Black woman can also persevere and there are still those who do their best to hold us back. I work hard every day for my family legacy and the legacy of all Black people. The list of empowered and dynamic Black women can never be too long. We do not have to be a First Lady, an entertainment and philanthropic billionaire, one of corporate America's most prominent executives, or an intelligent and athletic phenom to make a difference. Do not be misled into complacency and satisfaction when you hear those incredible names. But do feel inspired to have a sense of urgency and agency with your most inner-felt callings. Add your own name to the list, so you can then serve as a lighthouse for those traveling the path behind you.

I learned a long time ago to be ten steps ahead and to always try to be prepared. Despite being let go from Dr. Stuey's medical facility, I carried on and continued to prosper through the numerous other medical facilities with which I had great relationships. God never fails.

N ot six months after I was dismissed in that most unthoughtful way, I received a call from that facility's former CEO.

"Hey Doc, I hope you are doing well and that the babies are growing fine. I want to share with you that since you left there has been a few issues going on."

"Doing fine, thanks for asking. Issues?"

"Yes. Not long after you left, the new CEO left, as well as the physiatrist that Dr. Stuey replaced you with. Doc, the staff misses you and wants you back. I completely understand if you say 'No'."

I thought about what Dr. Stuey did to me, then I remembered all the things that my friend the former CEO and his staff had done for me.

I humbly answered him, "When do I start?"

In the wise words of my Forever First Lady, Michelle Obama, "When they go low, we go high."

9

Martin vs. Malcolm

"Hope is not a plan."
- Anderson Cooper

Throughout my entire career, I have done my best to take a higher road in the face of obstacles that were rooted in racism or sexism. I have understood that regardless of how insensitive the action of marginalization or unfair treatment is, the response of those marginalized has to be the opposite: We must think deeply about what we are going to say or do when addressing the offense, lest we can endanger ourselves or our careers. It is as if how we acknowledge the experience holds greater weight than the original offense. "It is not what happens to you, it is how you handle what happens to you that matters most." I have heard this time and time again. We are always being tested to determine our strength of character, and our responses give us the answers to who we really are. I choose to use the (Dr.) Martin (Luther King Jr.) vs Malcolm (X) approach. They were both powerful and effective leaders. Dr. King encouraged a calmer, peaceful form of expression while Mr. X encouraged people to act more aggressively when taking destiny into their own hands. For me to thrive with my career, I must know when to use what approach.

My experience with Dr. Stuey was more "Martin." I could have called him out for his blatant acts of sexism toward me; yet I chose to respond with modesty and class. And even after he cruelly discontinued my services at his facility for that period, I agreed to return when offered the opportunity by the former CEO because I held the bigger picture in mind. Dr. Stuey, despite still being the medical director of that facility, became irrelevant to me after that crass encounter with him. Despite what I knew he was about where I was concerned, the team provided a safe enough space for me to return to. There were amazing therapists, nurses, and administrative staff who I previously worked with and were always there for me. They respected what I brought to the table as a physician. Had I responded to Dr. Stuey with the same amount of arrogance and disdain he first shot at me, perhaps the second opportunity to be contracted at this facility never would have resurfaced. I found a way to work WITHIN the established system, which inspires me to think of Dr. Martin Luther King, Jr.

There are times that prove to be so toxic, however, that they are better handled with more of a "Malcolm X" approach: Maintain your integrity and eloquence, but unflinchingly speak your truth even if it makes others uncomfortable or unhappy. Such was the case with both The Practice and with The Agency. Both experiences undermined me in such egregious ways, and both were rooted in marginalization not just because of my gender, but also because of my race. Racial or gender discrimination is oftentimes a challenge to prove. However, if you feel in your heart what you are experiencing is based on race or gender, consider if it is best to remove yourself from the environment. When you feel the discrimination will not go away or appears to be escalating to the point of becoming a risk to your career or even your physical safety, it may be best to leave. Only you will know if you should remain and try to make a difference within or if you should part ways. For me, it was the latter. In both of those circumstances, I might have had an angel or two who were willing to provide me information to help confirm some facts. In the end, I did not believe their support was put in place so I should remain there. There was no safe space in either situation. I was determined to do what was best for me, my family, and my career. So, everything that detailed my decision to leave had to be rooted with the same level of resoluteness and proactive measures. The disrespect I was shown at The Practice and The Agency ensured my unwillingness to ever work with them again, and my resignation letter to The Practice was straight to the point. It read:

To the Physicians at The Practice,

At this point due to the particularly hostile and threatening interactions initiated and perpetuated by your staff, I am submitting my contractual 90-day notice.

Thank you for the opportunity,

Dr. Kimberly Gilbert

There are other ways in which I have had to use "my versions" of the Martin versus Malcom approach when speaking up, demanding respect, and taking my career into my own hands, determining at each moment which approach would be in the best interests of my Big Picture. Even speaking my truth in this book exemplifies this. By sharing with you some key moments in my life, regardless of how up or down, that have worked together to help move me forward is my way of encouraging anyone who might be going through similar trials so you know you are not alone. While building my career, there were no easily accessible transparent, honest, and uninhibited perspectives of Black female physicians who could help me navigate obstacles. I didn't even meet a "real life" Black female physician until I was in my third year of medical school. I know I am not alone in this. Your situation may not be exactly like mine, but you may have a similar feeling about whatever you are aspiring to or going through. I hope to provide something tangible and supportive for anyone feeling like there is no one around you who "gets it." Believe me, I get it. I get YOU.

My bold move of no longer working full-time for anyone else has proven to be the best choice for me. Aside from being a hard-working physician, I have also developed my enterprising skills along the way, and I learned I can be my own boss. And I love it!

Being on my own allows me to focus on my work more, which is what I had been preparing to do for so many years. I don't have to spend unnecessary time having to share details about my personal life or engaging in irrelevant gossip or other small talk just to "fit in." My track record, work ethic, professionalism, and cordial demeanor should always speak for themselves, and these attributes combined is what should be putting a medical team, and patients, at ease.

While having autonomy though, I am not exempt from marginalization — my Dr. Stuey experience occurred while I served as an independent consultant, and, when I chose to leave The Agency, I was also not an employee. I agreed to be aligned with them, as they promised to help steer and create opportunities for me as an independent contractor.

So... When Do I See the Doctor?

Being an independent contractor, I am not protected from the daily ridiculous, audacious, and cutting, "Sooooo...when do I see the doctor?" comments, and I am not shielded from other forms of unfair opposition and detractors. I did not become an entrepreneur believing it would spare me from discrimination. It does, however, give me an added peace of mind about how in control I can be regarding my career.

Whether working independently or as part of a team, it is my responsibility to be in control of ME.

As women, we must also know how to guard ourselves against certain men who offer "business opportunities" but request to do so over dinner, drinks, or other "set up" situations to mask their mal-intent. If you are unsure whether you are being targeted, I find it wise to have someone you trust accompany you to the "meeting." I have no hesitation including my husband in any off-hours "business opportunity" meetings. If the intent is innocent, there should be no push back.

You be in control of YOU.

I still enter environments where people behave in ways to belittle my hard work and achievements. I am often called "Miss" or "Miss Kimberly" or "Miss Gilbert" as opposed to "Doctor," no matter how my name appears on my name tag they stared at right before calling me anything but what they read.

Over the years, my embroidered lab coat or stainless-steel name tag has read, "Kimberly Gilbert MD," "Dr. Kimberly Gilbert," "Dr. Kimberly Gilbert, MD," "Dr. Gilbert," and "Dr. Gilbert, MD." The most recent version is "Dr. Gilbert, Physician."

With this latest unmistakable version, I am often asked, "What's your first name?"

"Kimberly."

"Okay, Kimberly. What were you saying?"

I have tried them all, and the truth is, if someone wants to demean you, regardless of knowing exactly what and who you are, they will try. Surprisingly perhaps, this treatment not only comes from people who do not look like me, but also from those who do. I could be in a room full of White male medical professionals and the other physicians, nurses, nurse's aides, and more would assume the White males were doctors, and I was not. The bias can be incredible. Medicine is a more diverse field today, and the face of physicians has long evolved from the bespectacled, aging White male clutching a black medical bag. There are times when medical staff in certain facilities choose to address me as a doctor. However, their follow-up question is one they need to ask in order to confirm I can practice as a physician because, in their eyes, a male doctor must lead me. "Dr. Gilbert, do you work for (insert male doctor's name here)?" It is unfortunate; there are still those who refuse to acknowledge times have changed.

It can be unnerving when I have spent real time with a patient and I am later asked by someone on staff, like a supervisor, if I have actually seen a certain patient because that patient would say things like, "I have never met a Dr. Gilbert," when I always make it my business to speak clearly upon entering each patient's room. These same patients would mention, "Oh, but I do love this one nurse practitioner/therapist/nurse/aide," later finding out that they were referring to me. Just not "My doctor." When I would kindly remind them that I was Dr. Gilbert, they would often say, "I really never thought you were actually a doctor. You don't look like a DOCTOR."

For people of color who keep up their own level of self-demoralization, it is disheartening that they, in similar and different ways than White people, do not think higher of us to address one another in ways that affirm our proper level of progress. I cannot count the number of times I have overheard Black patients and even fellow Black people in my facilities as well as my community speaking about White doctors or other professionals, "Oh, he's White so he's good." For a moment, I forget what year it is. Better yet, what decade.

It is unfortunate that too many of the marginalized fall victim to the lower stereotypes about themselves so much that they believe these horrific labels, which keep them limited while also making them impediments to the progress of those of us who are actually trying to break through barriers. There are times when women do not align with other women in professional settings, believing that having stronger alliances with their male colleagues will be more valuable for them. There are Black people who side with various forms of racial oppression, often encouraging those who experience it to be quiet and grateful "because it could be worse," or they actually think that fellow hard-working Black people who experience any discrimination somehow have themselves to blame.

I will never swallow the pill that encourages me to play the "grateful" role all while being taken advantage of. I know I will find strong alliances should I feel the need to stand up for my rights. And being particularly aligned with fellow women who are moving in the same direction of growth, success, and possibility could never lessen how solid I am perceived to be. I appreciate all the men who have been and continue to be a part of my support team, but the women who stand for me on the front lines of my village take me to an even higher level.

While we know that character traits like being compassionate, strong, or simply holding our heads high help make us whole, others will try to flip them into negative stereotypes of being "emotional," a "bitch," or believing that we are "better than" someone else. Thankfully, I know myself enough — and hopefully you do too — not to allow any of those efforts to matter.

I am proud of myself for achieving my goal of becoming a physician. I am proud to represent my family with this achievement, my gender with this achievement, and especially because of the constant negative depictions perpetuated about us every day, I feel proud to represent Black people. Yet not all Black people are proud I made it. I shake my head when I hear the distant chatter from some Black people about how I arrived at my position, attributing my external as if my career is not 100% brain dependent:

"She got that because she's cute."

"She got that because she's light-skinned with long hair."

Let's be clear: Cute doesn't save patients' lives — knowledge does.

From grand gestures to the up close and personal, all of it sometimes leaves me feeling disenchanted, knowing that mainstream society has successfully inspired drama intra-racially and intra-culturally. Divide and conquer at its best.

The idea of constantly having to prove myself can be exhausting. I thank God for the continued patience I have been given to cope with all of this, and despite the clouds manufactured by others, my eternal sunshine derives from knowing I have an extraordinary gift to share with the world every day. My mere presence and work, even if whatever race or gender or ethnicity of people refuse to acknowledge my medical contributions, is celebrated daily by each patient who makes physical progress with my expertise. This is one of the reasons why I chose to become a medical doctor. I feel confident enough within to never allow anyone to impose their negative energy on me, and no one can take away the joy I feel each time I am able to make a difference in someone's life.

I have also been through enough in my career and life to not need to be enlisted as anyone's token Black female at any organization to help them "check a box" or maintain a status within the industry. From my experience at The Practice, I learned I could never be the safe player who will accept any downgrading to be well paid. When I took a chance on myself and became independent, the number of those who reached for me and my expertise blew me away — especially because now I could engage on my own terms. I learned I could shine bright with autonomy and develop a community based on mutual respect and integrity. There was no looking back.

With so many stories to tell, (there are countless more), what I hope you can take away from my journey is an encouraging voice to access your inner ability to stay grounded and focused throughout your own career and life growth.

These affirmations I hold dear and have helped me along the way. I hope they do the same for you:

1. Know your **WORTH**: Silence any doubt within and understand how valuable you are. This helps you determine what you will not compromise on whenever you're navigating what I call, "people being people" as they undervalue you every chance they get, often boldly and unashamed, and particularly heightened at

certain times. Knowing your worth also gives you a sense of calm when people offend you, and that "calm" enables you to make the appropriate decision for the situation, whatever that means. It helps you understand the difference between helpful critique and learning opportunities versus actual discrimination and denigration. It also gives you the power of discernment to know who to listen to, when to listen to them, and what lessons the experience with them can teach you.

2. Know your **CRAFT**: Be the best you can at whatever it is you do. To know your craft means going the distance to reach the summit of your journey. Do not skip steps and skim your process. Take it all the way. Jessica Yourko said, "Have enough courage to start and enough heart to finish." When you own your craft, no one will be able to take that away from you. People will always offer unsolicited criticisms and speak disparagingly about someone or something; true excellence unveils the real nature of their intent, which then makes their comments irrelevant. Knowing your craft also creates more financial opportunities because people will seek your expertise/talent/product/service knowing they will receive the highest level of quality. And perhaps most importantly, your craft will help you win your "end game," which, for me, is to provide my family, loved ones, and those who come after me with more opportunities for happiness and success that do not require them to lower their standards or expectations to accommodate someone else because they feel they "need" them.

3. Know your **BOUNDARIES**: Create your "safe space" which consists of your mental, physical, and emotional cores. This safe space has no one else in it because you have to remember it is

possible that the person closest to you may be the one to hurt you, so you always have to have a place of self-protection, self-preservation, and refuge within. Our children mean the world to us, but as children grow to be adults they develop their own opinions, values, and behaviors that could be misaligned with our own, and while we love them with all of our hearts and then some, we still deserve an inner space designed for ourselves. It doesn't mean we abandon them; it just means we are not "broken" by their actions. The same goes for a spouse or partner. Just outside of your core is a cherished layer comprised of people who are the most meaningful to you, like the family you were birthed into, the family you created, friends "like family," and so on. Next, would be remaining friends, then acquaintances and colleagues, all forming sequentially more distant layers from your core like the rings around Saturn. Remember, allow people in only to the degree of your proven connection with them. A colleague could have a stronger connection with you than someone who considers them-selves your friend, or a friend may be more loyal to you than "family," so do not get caught up in labels and titles. Make sure that the outermost layer is comprised of those with a tendency to try to bring you down in any way. Keep them far, far away from your precious core.

4. Know your **BALANCE**: Keep current who and what keeps you leveled. Just as important as the types of food you eat, the amount of water you drink, how much sleep you need to be optimally productive, it is equally important to get your daily dose of emotional nutrition from those you respect and love, and mini-mize or avoid internalizing virulent energy or dialogue from infec-tive people. Knowing your balance will alert your receptors to

noxious stimuli even if you do not exactly know what is going on yet. The initial "feeling" will help you move toward attaining the clarity or understanding needed to decide what to do next.

I encourage you to consider these four staples for your own life. They may also help you move through your journey without any feelings of resentment or bitterness, because you will have learned to own and understand your process. From them, I have formed my "Teflon Skin" which makes many of the unfair judgements, attacks, or biases that have come my way slide right off.

All things considered, even if you do not commit to this brand of wisdom, still know I believe you can create your own affirmations to keep your eye on the ultimate prize, even if there are seeming failures along the way.

Michael Jordan once said, "I've missed over 9,000 shots in my career, I've lost almost 300 games. Twenty-six times, I've been trusted to take the game winning shot and missed. I've failed over and over and over again in my life. And that is why I succeed."

Right now, we are in the midst of a global pandemic with COVID-19. While this has slowed much of our economy and travel, the stay-at-home orders issued around the world made it, so we had ample time to reflect on our current state and initiate needed change. For the first time in recent history, the effects of this coronavirus have made it so we are not able to be distracted by the usual hobbies and leisure activities that could turn our eyes away from the horrific racial injustices in the world that have been going on for far too many years. The forced isolation gave us the chance to fully process what is deeply affecting all of us from the varying angles of life. There were no live sporting events, no current reality TV shows, no concerts, no conferences, or other large gatherings to escape reality, even if for only a couple of hours, an injustice we witnessed either on the television or in real life. The stay-at-home order kept us inside of our homes, and either alone or in small groups, we thought about it. We still think about it. If the news reports the latest social injustice, we do not casually take it in and out while getting dressed in our favorite outfit to go out to dinner or a nightclub. Instead, we listen intently to the details, going through a myriad of emotions about what we just heard. "Facts do not cease to exist because we choose to ignore them," and now more than ever, the facts are penetrating our hearts as a collective world. Many hard truths and inequities are being brought to light, such as age-old efforts to enhance the barriers of separation between races and cultures. Being brought more to the forefront is the intent of these barriers of separation, which is to keep some of us out of the realms of positive opportunity, and it leaves us unshielded from the dangers in the world. Black and Brown people are being murdered everyday as an example of those hard truths of racism that are being brought more into focus. To date, the pandemic home quarantine has highlighted many of the latest racially motivated murders of Black and Brown people, all under different circumstances, mostly at the hands of White people, often wearing a badge. Now more than ever, it is important for Black and Brown people to know the power we hold within to be our strongest, so we can thrive. If you are not Black or Brown but hold a position to assist and serve as an ally, help make someone else's journey be safer and richer. Regardless of who you are, you owe it yourself and to the world around you to treat everyone with respect and equality.

If you are reading this book, I believe you are someone who appreciates living consciously and on purpose. Elevate your purpose and push the envelope of equity and equality FORWARD.

10

The Great Relay

"Let us run with perseverance the race marked out for us."
- Hebrews 12:1 NIV

Being fully valued for who you are and for what you bring to the table by the world around you would be a most marvelous way of life, I can imagine. I believe when you are being valued in this capacity it creates a self-sustaining, just, supportive, and thriving community you can always depend on. You can then return the favor and respect others the same. Anything less begets an imbalanced community, where some people feel better about themselves than others, a world where lack of appreciation can lead to lack of ambition and creativity. This kind of community is filled with instability, where some get a good life and others do not. And it is largely based upon an overall choice to take part in, or equally as bad, even tolerate, racism and inequality toward certain people.

Though the second, unstable "community" I describe resembles more of the world in which we live today, those of us who recognize the disparities and injustices have the ability to improve our communities, demand equality and equity where these problems exist, and also choose to lead our own lives with fairness and harmony to reflect that which we seek — i.e., "Be the change we would like to see in the world."

Being a Black female physician has, in a great way, attracted for me a wealth of positivity and purpose. Yet, it has also brought on a number of detractors and critics, people who would rather demean than uplift my work, "professional" environments that are filled with staff who undermine and are insubordinate all because they feel resentment for the color of my skin and the medical position I hold. Patients who refuse to believe I am equally as capable of caring for them as my White counterparts, some patients even refusing to receive any care at all if it required for me to treat them. All because of the race and gender that God chose me to be. As I grow in my craft, I have gone through my share of wisdom-building trials to arrive where I stand today. And while being humbled along the way, my sense of empowerment has only widened and deepened, this as a result of earning a level of independence that has allowed me to beat to my own drum while working within the medical system. To have achieved fundamental autonomy is beneficial for someone like me because with it, there is less chance someone will try to shortchange me for my work, and less chance I will receive biased treatment because I am Black or female. Though I say, "less chance," I cannot fully prevent such treatment.

I think about my precious twin daughters, who will one day be mature enough to lead lives of their own. It is my hope that by the time they get there I, and others like me, will have created a world where they will have the choice not to have to work with people who discriminate against them the same way I have been or worse, and have certainty that wherever they work is inclusive of true allies, particularly where White people are concerned.

I believe this is possible because there was a time when Black people were penalized for wanting to learn how to read, and our ancestors pushed tirelessly so the generations following them could educate themselves as freely as they chose — and it worked. In a heartbeat, I would readily give my life for my family. And by the way I navigate the life I lead now by gaining wisdom, opportunities, and stability for them, I realize I already am.

Thinking back to the life I led decades ago, how I had the opportunity to be educated in two different settings, first attending an HBCU and later PWIs, I recall that any real level of anxiety about who I was and what I could bring to the table began when I left the fold of those who looked like me. Yes, Mr. George's words from high school, "You are not smart enough to be a doctor," stung me deeply. But as Johnny Depp once said, "One day the people that didn't believe in you will tell everyone how they met you."

Mr. George was a Black man, but I am thankful I have had many other Black men whose influences in my life swatted this one unsupportive teacher's perspective like a mosquito in the middle of summer. Mr. George had no real weight up against the army of Black men who would have also stepped to him if I had told any of them back then the vicious words he spoke to me. Mr. George held such little prominence in my grand scheme of things, that by the time I was set to encounter the Napoleon-complexed medical director, Dr. Stuey, who also happened to be a Black man, his words to me felt nonsensical, and I blew them away as easily as one blows out a candle. Dr. Stuey's perspective was never considered or given light.

The Black women who come and go, who feel the need to give me what they would believe to be sage advice to be "grateful," to "play your role," and "don't complain" when I am being discriminated against by someone who is White or male, as if I have no right to demand equal pay and treatment for my level of credentials as well as who I present myself to be every single day — I almost feel sorry for these women. I sometimes wonder if, along their journeys, someone was not keen on showing them their worth enough that they could not later recognize my plight as their own. But for every "lost" Black woman I encounter, I have legions of "found" ones, who are beautiful in every way. They are proud and successful. They are on conscious paths to create change for the better. I have a powerful village of Black people around me who uphold me at all costs so the adversity within my own culture overall feels minimal.

When I stepped out of the space with those who did not look like me, I felt like I was walking uphill carrying my race (and at times, my gender) like sandbags tied to my ankles. Being Black and female was often not a thing to be celebrated. These were attributes I had to constantly defend in some way. I have had many experiences where there was no one willing to serve as an ally to support or defend me despite secretly agreeing that I was being unfairly treated or judged. At best, they would turn a blind eye to not seem controversial, and maybe one or two would overcompensate by being nice to me to make up for all the dis-crimination they ignored in our work environment. As for patients, how do you correct someone who is discriminating against you while you are simultaneously improving, and sometimes literally saving, their lives?

There are countless times when I must swallow the bitter pill of prejudice or contention to go on and execute what is right. All patients deserve my absolute best if they are in need. I pride-fully serve those whose personalities are not as desired, as well as the helpless patients who have inspired hard-hearted looks toward me by staff because those patients were underprivileged and did not have good health insurance, if they had any at all. These patients were often people of color. For example, as a physiatrist, there have been a significant number of Black patients I have encountered in my career undergoing rehabilitation due to a potentially debilitating condition known as peripheral vascular disease (PVD). At an alarmingly disproportionate rate, these patients were recommended to have their limb(s) amputated versus their White counterparts, who were more often offered limb-saving treatment plans. I would also see Black patients who had unfortunately suffered a cerebrovascular accident (CVA, or stroke), and their physician hospital discharge orders would read: "Transfer patient to nursing home's next available bed for permanent placement — poor rehab potential" while White stroke patients with the same diagnosis and functional level were given discharge orders that read: "Transfer patient to acute inpatient rehabilitation to receive intensive physical, occupational, and speech therapies in order to maximize their outcomes – good rehab potential." There is no question that God kept me on this path to medicine so that I could be an eye and a voice for vulnerable people. I took an oath as a physician, and every chance I get I try to prevent as many patients as I can from "dying from being Black." Those who choose to deny people in need can take it up with their god that they turned a blind eye, and I will happily testify to mine that I chose not to.

I have made the decision time and time again to forgo a lucrative opportunity or a more prestigious in-house title when I felt signing on the bottom line would go against my sense of integrity. Many of these "key" moments of discernment at this stage of my career can have me leap in any direction, and these leaps will affect my beloved daughters. I want them to know that although their mom was not always first, she stood for something, and because of it, ended up holding the real prize: The badge of self-preservation and self-respect. I teach them that sacrificing for the right reasons will always pay off, even in this world, and being "the best" is only about doing your best. All of my work and efforts are for my family, and if my daughters take heed to my life and career as an example of how to win by remaining true to themselves, I look forward to the day when I get to give them birthday cards that read the same as the ones that my parents gave to me as a teenager, inscribed with something like, "One day, you will have the opportunity to feel the same love and pride we do."

I t takes a lot for anyone to aspire to greatness. Black people are treated on face value — guilty until proven innocent, undervalued, and underestimated with how smart we are and how successful we can become. It takes triple the amount of hope, perseverance, grit, and courage for a Black person to have these kinds of dreams. Add being a woman to the equation, and the dream can sometimes seem impossible. I, Dr. Kimberly Gilbert, a proud Black woman, will continue to push forward in the face of the adversity. At each level of achievement I am able to earn, I strengthen more inside. This inner strength fortifies the platform of opportunity and choice that I am building for my daughters as well as all others who come after me.

For all those people who don't look like me and try to stand in my way to make my road harder, I continue to smile and serve as the best physician I can be. To me, these people are "blind on purpose." And while I do not know a substantial enough number of White people who have the visual acuity to offset the others, it is not my responsibility to be their "Black friend" and help them figure out why they cannot seem to look at Black people as full, equally deserving human beings. Furthermore, I am not here to help them understand why their thoughts and actions scream "Privilege." It shouldn't take anyone else for them to realize something so fundamental: that everyone, regardless of race, desires and deserves to have the same safety, respect, and opportunities as they do.

There are seas of good, incredibly gifted, and magnificent Black people in this world. Those who are "purposefully blind" have the choice to appreciate impressive Black people each time they see them but instead decide to cheapen them in every encounter. Despite it all, I remain resolute to rise above the hate, do great work, and not require any approval from bigots.

Whose opinions and feelings I do highly regard are those coming from the people who have invested in me from the moment we were brought together, like my tried-and-true family and friends, who also understand some level of marginalization in both similar and different ways than my experiences.

I think of my big sister, Ericka, a solid and intelligent Black woman, and a kick-ass attorney. She had to ascend to her success while being discriminated against for her race, her gender, and her sexual orientation. My sister rode every wave and stands amazing and tall. Even my husband, John, has gone through his share of experiences with marginalization. He makes our family especially proud as a former professional athlete and as a successful entrepreneur. I recall the racist reporter who warned that LeBron James should just "shut up and dribble," and how LeBron responded to her insensitive and ignorant comments with positive action.[13] "King James" exemplifies how athletes can excel with achievements based on intellect and not just physical prowess, whether by opening a school in his hometown or the many other phenomenal and influential contributions he continues to make to the Black community. Success will always be the best revenge.

"Success no matter what or who" could be my motto and the motto for everyone I know who made it not because of, but in spite of. As Black people, we might never be able to fully escape the bull's eye target of discrimination, marginalization, and blatant racism in our lives. We can, however, create a world within a world where what matters most is what we feel about ourselves and our loved ones, and the opinions of the rest of the world we will cease to hear. Those who choose to remain blind will have that option, but those who are willing to open their eyes will see our excellence and want to align themselves with the greatness we create. My husband and I affirm our daughters every single day, as do the other core adults in their lives serving as a village to help shape them as human beings and as future women. I know that what is focused on expands, and armed with the right mindset, sense of confidence, and as much of a head start as my husband and I can provide, the sky will be the limit for them. The late Whitney Houston — "The Voice" — sang it best: "Learning to love yourself, it is the greatest love of all."

When you love yourself, you demand respect from those unwilling to give it on their own. My mother and father ensured that I loved myself, and that self-love keeps me intolerant of other people's ill intentions in any form. I can testify that it is an extraordinary thing.

Our self-love is particularly important as Black people because so much of the world around us does not bestow it to us. We have been shown through generations of oppression like slavery, denial of the right to vote, then later voter suppression, redlining, forced segregation, unequal educational opportunities, and police killings of unarmed Black people. When it comes to our basic human rights, it matters not the level of degree earned, the title within one's career and diversity of our talents and range of success, or how much money we may hold in our bank account, we are still seen as one blurred block of people. According to many White people in this country and in the world, the common phrase "they all look alike," historically applies to Black people. In the eyes of those purposefully blind and ignorant people, nothing we accomplish as Black people will render us worthy of full humanity in their eyes. Black people are a complex people. And even though there are those of us who have pressed upon society that we are not a monolith and to be seen or considered as one thing lumped into the category of "lazy, undereducated, or non-achieving" people, when it comes to our human rights as a people, we unite as one.

When we learn of a serious infraction that has happened to someone in our community, many of us can quickly relinquish that mentality of individuality for the sake of standing up for our own. For centuries we have done this: We marched in the 1960s for civil rights, largely inspired by one African American woman, Rosa Parks, who was unjustly arrested in 1955 for refusing to give up her seat to a White passenger on a city bus.[14] Today, we are called to rise again. The recent COVID-19 global pandemic has illuminated the racial and socioeconomic disparities that have plagued the Black community for centuries. Unemployment due to

151

the pandemic is greatest seen in the industries that typically employ a high percentage of Black people. One of the highest percentages of hospitalizations and deaths due to COVID-19 is occurring in the Black population, particularly Black men. [15] [16] [17] [18]

When society wants to blame us for having "so many underlying health conditions and living in poor neighborhoods" that put us at risk for higher morbidity and mortality, they forget that, for centuries, we have been denied proper healthcare that could prevent us from developing certain health issues or at least be better able to manage them. They forget we have been denied educational and vocational opportunities that could help us acquire the knowledge or skillsets to obtain safer, higher paying occupations, that would then afford us the opportunity to live in "better" neighborhoods. They forget how this country disproportionately incarcerates Black people, who, if or when they are finally released, then have the near-hopeless undertaking of obtaining legitimate job opportunities. They forget that we were first denied the right to vote at all, and when they could no longer get away with that, they indirectly got the same result through voter suppression. And then, there is the most brazenly fatalistic part of their plan:

"Hell, just kill 'em because what are they going to do about it anyway?"

The impact of the most recent publicized fatalities has urged Black people and some non-Black allies to come together, this time, with the world feeling a unified pain. These painful, traumatic, and unjust losses of life for these Black human beings at the hands of White people who so callously sought out to destroy Black people has rocked our complacent world.

The first filmed hate crime we saw during this pandemic was Ahmaud Arbery, a young Black man who was shot and killed in cold blood by a deadly trio consisting of a thug-like former cop, his son, and another accomplice filming the tragic event, all White.[19] A second heartbreaking tragedy involved the killing of Breonna Taylor, who was shot and killed in her home while sleeping after police officers raided her home. This incident was not filmed but was obviously merciless and criminal.[20] The third of this string of devastating events was another filmed tragedy, and as a nation, we witnessed in horror as George Floyd, an unarmed Black man, was suffocated by a White police officer who placed his knee upon George's neck for nearly NINE minutes while George cried out, "I can't breathe."[21] Rayshard Brooks died fleeing from police in an Atlanta Wendy's restaurant parking lot after he fell asleep in the drive-thru lane.[22] Then there are the Black people who have recently been discovered around the country hanging by their necks and labeled as "suicides."[23] Many Black people are rightfully suspicious of this because of the long history of the lynching of Black people in this country[24], many of those also labeled as suicides despite clear evidence that it was impossible for the victim to have done so.

Simple acts like walking in your own neighborhood, going to the grocery store or out to eat at a restaurant, even just heading to work generates anxiety because you don't know what — better yet who — could happen. Christian Cooper was enjoying his day birdwatching in Central Park when he politely asked a White lady, Amy Cooper, to follow park rules and put a leash on her dog.[25] Amy instinctively knew to unleash possibly the deadliest weapon in the history of our country: The White woman's tears. It has been the cause of death for an incalculable number of Black people, usually Black men, with one of the most historic tragedies related to it being Emmett Till, a 14-year-old Black boy in Mississippi who was beaten, mutilated, shot in the head, and thrown into the river after he was accused of flirting with a White woman in her family's grocery store.[26]

The endless list of tragedies is not just heartbreaking, it is sickening. In the minds and hearts of our community — doctors, lawyers, teachers, "essential workers," pastors, students, stay-at-home moms and dads, grandparents, and everyone else — are all linking arms in protest against police brutality towards Black people and any other forms of racial injustices, and we stand connected and unbreakable in support of equality and equity for us.

As Black people, we stand united for a progression that we as a people have long deserved to be entitled to as citizens of this country. When one of us wins, we all feel the triumph. At the same time, when one of us loses, as a community, we feel the loss in ways untold. The scientific argument that we carry trauma in our DNA throughout generations continues to be examined deeper. Our common thread of spirit will make it so that even those of us who consciously choose not to get in the ring will still feel the punch deep down inside. We were stolen and misled from our homeland and brought to America and other places in groups. Separated from our families, children ripped from their mothers and fathers, husbands and wives broken apart. And though not physically able to always be together, the spirit of Black people will remain connected and unbroken. God bless the motherless child.

To that end, I believe that as with everything, it will be our spirits and our hearts that will help us get to the finish line. For centuries we have been in a race for our lives, metaphorically and oftentimes, literally. We are in a race for equity, a race for equality, a race for life protection, a race for fair housing, a race for job opportunity, and a race for the best education. As a people, we have been in this relay race since before the Reconstruction[27], and with each movement thereafter we are passed batons, as the previous generation has propelled Black people closer towards the finish line of full equality. My ancestors earnestly ran their leg of the race and passed the baton down the line to their children, and so on until the baton passed to my parents. When my parents were ready to pass the baton to us to improve on what they had set up for my sister and me, we were given the understanding first that our lives are to be lived as legs of the Great Relay Race, and we were encouraged to run our hardest and smartest. We were told that this relay race would be highly unfair at times, that there would be sabotage, but we owed it to ourselves, and those who come after us, not to quit. Paolo Coelho wrote,

"You drown not by falling in the river, but by staying submerged in it."

So, not if but when there are actions made to cripple or disqualify our own noble missions, we must keep going no matter what.

We were reminded that our parents and others had achieved their part of getting us as far as they had done, as their parents had done for them, and it was our turn to make this next leg count. I am grateful to say with all the powerful wisdom bestowed to Ericka and me, we went racing towards our goals.

I have certainly lived my life as a relay race, and I proudly play my part in this feat for me and all my people. As an adult, I entered the race focused on the Big Win. I am confident because I have been thoroughly prepared for this moment:

I began my jog in position, patiently waiting yet eager for my turn at the handoff. As the time approached, I paced forward to keep up with the momentum then threw my hand back. As the baton was being placed into my open palm, I heard the code word telling me that my time had come. I secured the baton and sprinted forward...

I felt the wind of progression that has already been achieved to advance us as a people, and with that energy and spirit behind me, I began to run this race with all my might.

In the distance, I see my two daughters, who John and I are raising to be even stronger than us, who will have been fully prepped and will be ready, like Olympic gold medalist Florence "Flo Jo" Griffith Joyner. Our daughters, like "Flo Jo", will have to know their winds and what surrounds them, all while staying laser focused. Our daughters will be in heavy anticipation for the baton to be passed on to them so they can then run their leg of the relay. It is my prayer that if our current generation cannot accomplish the ultimate victory of equality and equity, my children's generation will succeed in crossing that great finish line.

You got this. We have so many examples of those who personify encouragement and promise to confirm what is possible for Black people to achieve.

Head up!

Don't stop!

Keep pushing!

Know that you have the patience and emotional fortitude of Nelson Mandela, the vision of Oprah Winfrey, the focus of Kobe Bryant, the strategy and perseverance of Harriet Tubman, the intelligence and class of Barack and Michelle Obama, and the strength and bravery of Lawrence Joel. And countless others. Remember who is in you.

This is why you can win.

And when you have finished running the race marked out for you, know that no matter what, by giving your all, you make us proud.

Photographic Memories

Mom, Dad, Me & Ericka

My sister Ericka & I

Me & My Horse Beauty

My Dad & I

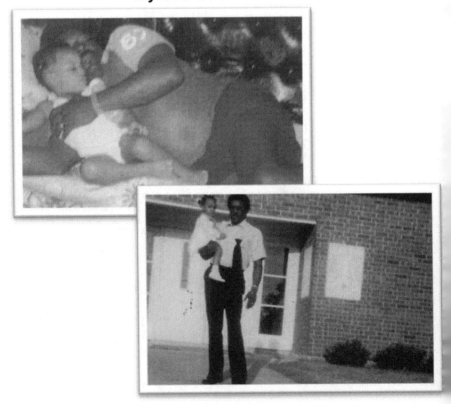

Top left to right: **Shae, Mom, Aunt Tru,**
Grandma Howard
Bottom left to right: **Ericka, Me**

Aunt Fritz & I

1999 - Aunt Louise, Me, and
Aunt Tru at my graduation
from Southern University in
Baton Rouge, LA

Kimberly Gilbert, MD

2005 - Graduation from LSU School of Medicine

John & I – Dating Days

Residency Graduation 2009

John & I – Wedding Day

John & I

So... When Do I See the Doctor?

Our Girls:
Brooklyn (left)   Milan (right)

The Keiths

Acknowledgements

First and foremost, Thank You, God. Thank You. Thank You. Until my last breath, I thank You.

There are and have been countless people along my life's journey who serve positive purposes in my life, providing words of wisdom and encouragement or career opportunities. I thank you from the bottom of my heart for every kind word and supportive action that you have ever shown me.

To my family:

To my two little hurricanes, Milan, and Brooklyn: You are my inspiration. Mommy loves you always.

To my incredible parents in Heaven, Coach Elliott Gilbert, and Mrs. Dorothea Gilbert: Not one day passes that I do not miss you but also thank God for allowing me to have you as my parents. I would not be who I am today without you.

I honor my wonderful husband, John Keith, who is my best friend and teammate. Thank you for being there whenever I need your love, thoughts, strength, or sometimes just your ear. You always support my dreams. You are a source of warmth and sunshine, and you come ready with an umbrella on any rainy day.

To my blessing of a sister, Ericka Gilbert: My words for you are simple and say it all: You are My ROCK. Your wisdom and strength have been priceless over the years, and I see your same influence helping Elliott, Ethan, and Lauren already show signs of greatness.

To Aunt Truvesta "Tru" Johnson: You are the only woman besides my mother who was, and is, everything to me and showed me what class, intelligence, hard work, humility, grace, and beauty look like. You helped me in such a major way evolve into the woman I am today. I appreciate you and your mother, Grandma Howard (RIP), who I call "The Original."

To Aunt Louise, who showed me how to be tender: You are the sweetest, most nurturing woman, and I have so much reverence for you and how you cared for Mom in her last days.

To my Aunt Fritz who showed me how to be fierce and fly without being "loud": You are truly a phenomenal woman.

To my Aunt Myrtice and all my Gary, Indiana, people: You are family and community. When I was in Indiana, you made me still feel "home."

To Mrs. Hadnot: my godmother and first real-life image of a Black female entrepreneur, and to your son, Dexter Hadnot: you are truly a godbrother in every sense of the word. I love you both.

To Tyrone Grider: You are Family and nothing less. My dad thought of you like a son, and you will always be my brother.

To Patrick Stewart: You are my ACE. Love you always, my brother.

To Mr. Bob Adams: You evolved from "my husband's friend" to also becoming one of my own dearest friends: You are a true confidante and source of wisdom and encouragement.

To my other "Sisters":

To Dr. Candace White Jackson: I don't know if you could ever know how grateful I am for our sisterhood. Words could never do it justice. Your intelligence, beauty, strength, and grace are such an inspiration to me and countless others.

So... When Do I See the Doctor?

To Mrs. Peridot Davis Chambers: You are possibly the biggest heart I have ever met. You are tender but stand your ground. Humble, yet so amazing. I cherish our friendship.

To Mrs. Jovonne Harvey: You have been my "sister" since the day we met. Our friendship is invaluable to me.

To Dr. Tonya Hendricks: You are a brilliant, beautiful, loving, unforgettable Black female physician and one of my dearest friends that God took Home far too soon. I miss you so much.

To all my educational and professional allies, many of whom I am also lucky to call friends:

To Dr. MacArthur Baker: Thank you for being there for me since medical school, part of "The Committee". You are an amazing physician and a dear friend.

To Dean Beverly Wade: Thank you for the opportunity and thank you for what you have done for generations of Black collegians.

To Dr. Bryan Lewis: You are a rare breed of old-school sense of responsibility for helping the future succeed.

To Mr. Herbert Patton: Thank you for always being there for me throughout the years. Proud to call you a very dear friend.

To Ms. Miki DeJean and Dr. Amys Lang: You always looked out for me when you did not have to. I thank you for your wisdom, kind hearts, and uncompromising spirits.

To Mrs. Cynthia Sosa, who has been there since the girls were six months old: Sincere gratitude to you for caring for Milan, Brooklyn, Max, Rowdy, Niko, and Sammy as though they are your own.

To Mrs. Angela Williams Ba: Another brilliant, beautiful Black woman. You are a trusted friend and business partner.

To Mrs. Chrishaunda Lee Perez: Thank you for helping me take the experiences from my head and emotions from my heart and put them on paper, hopefully helping anyone else experiencing marginalization to feel supported and stay encouraged.

To Ms. Darlene Hollis: Thank you for educating and coaching me throughout the publishing process and continuing to support and encourage my independence as a new author. It speaks volumes how you always want the spotlight to shine on others.

To the Eastern Star Baptist Church in Indianapolis, IN, (Pastor Jeffrey Johnson) and Franklin Avenue Baptist Church in New Orleans, LA, (Pastor Fred Luter Jr.): I am grateful to all of you for providing a place of hope, guidance, and clarity, even during the darkest of times.

To Delta Sigma Theta Sorority, Incorporated: I thank you for what you have done for me and all aspiring Black women since January 13,1913. On so many levels, I greatly admire what the organization stands for and executes every day. I am a proud Soror.

SPECIAL LOVE to the Alpha Tau Chapter at Southern University in Baton Rouge, Louisiana.

I honor Dr. Keith Amos: My original real-life inspiration for believing I could ever become a physician. Rest in Power.

Bibliography

1. https://www.forbes.com/sites/lipiroy/2020/02/25/its-my-calling-to-change-the-statistics-why-we-need-more-black-female-physicians/#5d78e7c556a5
2. https://press-herald.com/new-book-tells-dr-keith-amos-story/
3. https://en.wikipedia.org/wiki/List_of_Delta_Sigma_Theta_sisters
4. https://pubmed.ncbi.nlm.nih.gov/30180066/
5. https://en.wikipedia.org/wiki/J._Marion_Sims
6. https://en.wikipedia.org/wiki/Tuskegee_syphilis_experiment
7. https://en.wikipedia.org/wiki/Henrietta_Lacks
8. https://en.wikipedia.org/wiki/Sarah_Baartman
9. https://www.britannica.com/biography/Daniel-Hale-Williams
10. https://en.wikipedia.org/wiki/Daniel_Hale_Williams
11. https://en.wikipedia.org/wiki/Rebecca_Lee_Crumpler
12. https://en.wikipedia.org/wiki/Timeline_of_Hurricane_Katrina
13. https://www.npr.org/sections/thetwo-way/2018/02/19/587097707/laura-ingraham-told-lebron-james-to-shutup-and-dribble-he-went-to-the-hoop
14. https://en.wikipedia.org/wiki/Rosa_Parks
15. https://www.cdc.gov/coronavirus/2019-ncov/community/health-equity/race-ethnici-ty.html?CDC_AA_refVal=https%3A%2F%2Fwww.cdc.gov%2Fcoronavirus%2F2019-ncov%2Fneed-extra-precautions%2Fracial-ethnic-minorities.html
16. https://www.npr.org/sections/health-shots/2020/05/30/865413079/what-do-coronavirus-racial-disparities-look-like-state-by-state

17. https://talkpoverty.org/basics/
18. https://www.ncbi.nlm.nih.gov/pmc/articles/PMC4817358/
19. https://en.wikipedia.org/wiki/Killing_of_Ahmaud_Arbery
20. https://en.wikipedia.org/wiki/Shooting_of_Breonna_Taylor
21. https://en.wikipedia.org/wiki/George_Floyd
22. https://en.wikipedia.org/wiki/Killing_of_Rayshard_Brooks
23. https://www.forbes.com/sites/tommybeer/2020/06/22/hanging-deaths-and-noose-sightings-raise-alarm-in-aftermath-of-george-floyd-protests/#eda599e1c1fb
24. https://en.wikipedia.org/wiki/Lynching_in_the_United_States
25. https://www.cnn.com/2020/05/26/us/central-park-video-dog-video-african-american-trnd/index.html
26. https://en.wikipedia.org/wiki/Emmett_Till
27. https://en.wikipedia.org/wiki/Reconstruction_era

About the Author

Kimberly Gilbert, MD

Dr. Kimberly Gilbert is a board-certified physician practicing in Atlanta, GA. She completed medical school at Louisiana State University School of Medicine in New Orleans, LA, before moving to Atlanta to complete a residency at Emory University in Physical Medicine and Rehabilitation. While thoroughly enjoying her medical role as a physiatrist in the rehabilitation of catastrophic illnesses and debilitating injuries, as well as being a diligent patient advocate, she has always had an equally passionate desire to help people achieve their vision of their "best self."

In addition to her professional responsibilities, Dr. Gilbert feels a social responsibility to help others. She does so by supporting several local and national organizations, with a passion for helping children, people with physical or mental disabilities, and rescued animals.

Dr. Gilbert owns several successful medical and aesthetic businesses in the Atlanta area, where she lives with her husband, twin daughters, three dogs, an aquarium full of fish, and an attack cat.

You can find out more about Kimberly Gilbert, MD at:
www.kimberlygilbertmd.com

Follow her on social media at
Facebook: @Kimberly Gilbert, MD
Instagram: @kimberlygilbertmd

Made in the USA
Columbia, SC
27 September 2020